HAN SOLO AND THE
HOLLOW MOON OF KHORYA

Designer
David Nestelle

Assistant Editor
Freddye Lins

Associate Editor
Dave Marshall

Editor
Randy Stradley

Publisher
Mike Richardson

special thanks to Elaine Mederer, Jann Moorhead, David Anderman,
Leland Chee, Sue Rostoni, and Carol Roeder at Lucas Licensing

STAR WARS ADVENTURES: HAN SOLO AND THE HOLLOW MOON OF KHORYA

ISBN: 9781845769055

Published by Titan Books, a division of Titan Publishing Group Ltd.
144 Southwark St, London, SE1 0UP

A CIP catalogue record for this title is available from the British Library.

First edition: March 2009

10 9 8 7 6 5 4 3 2 1

Printed in Lithuania

STAR WARS® ADVENTURES

HAN SOLO AND THE HOLLOW MOON OF KHORYA

Script Jeremy Barlow

Pencils Rick Lacy

Inks Matthew Loux

Colours Michael Atiyeh

Lettering Michael Heisler

Cover art Rick Lacy and Michael Atiyeh

TITAN BOOKS

THIS STORY TAKES PLACE APPROXIMATELY ONE YEAR BEFORE STAR WARS: A NEW HOPE.

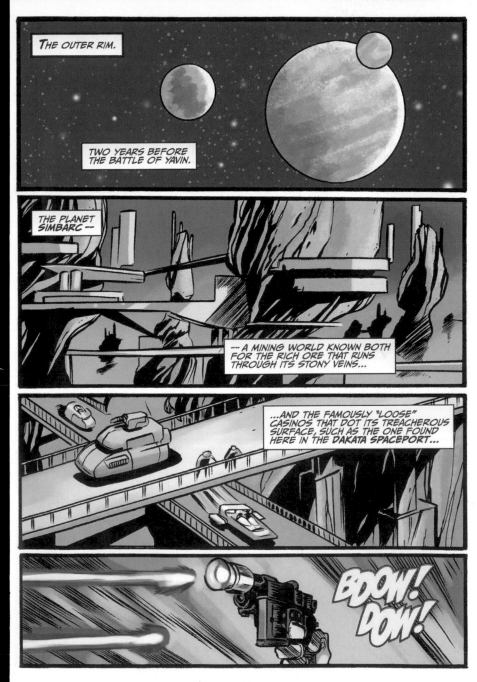

THE OUTER RIM.

TWO YEARS BEFORE THE BATTLE OF YAVIN.

THE PLANET SIMBARC --

-- A MINING WORLD KNOWN BOTH FOR THE RICH ORE THAT RUNS THROUGH ITS STONY VEINS...

...AND THE FAMOUSLY "LOOSE" CASINOS THAT DOT ITS TREACHEROUS SURFACE, SUCH AS THE ONE FOUND HERE IN THE DAKATA SPACEPORT...

BDOW!
DOW!

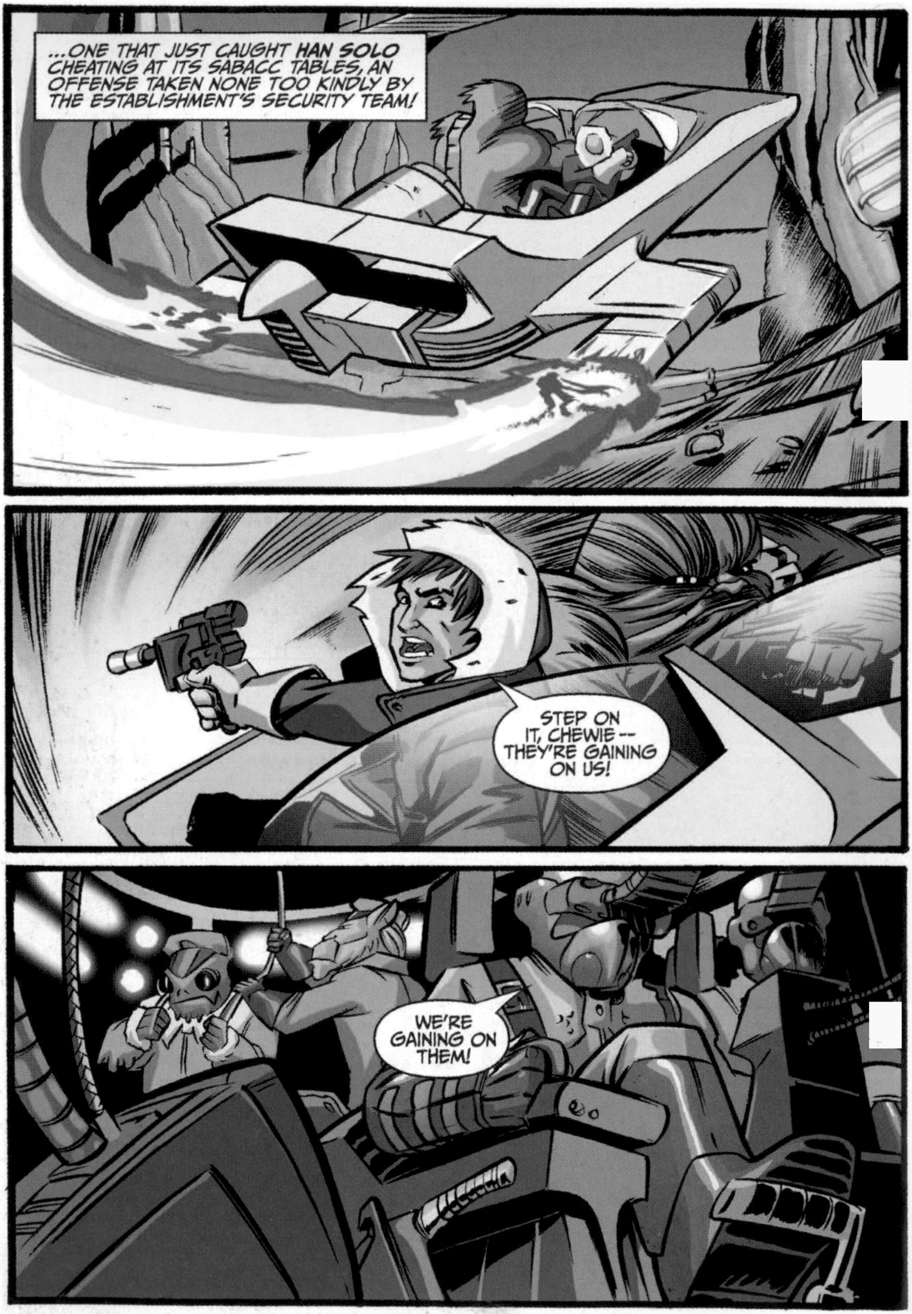
...ONE THAT JUST CAUGHT HAN SOLO CHEATING AT ITS SABACC TABLES, AN OFFENSE TAKEN NONE TOO KINDLY BY THE ESTABLISHMENT'S SECURITY TEAM!
STEP ON IT, CHEWIE -- THEY'RE GAINING ON US!
WE'RE GAINING ON THEM!

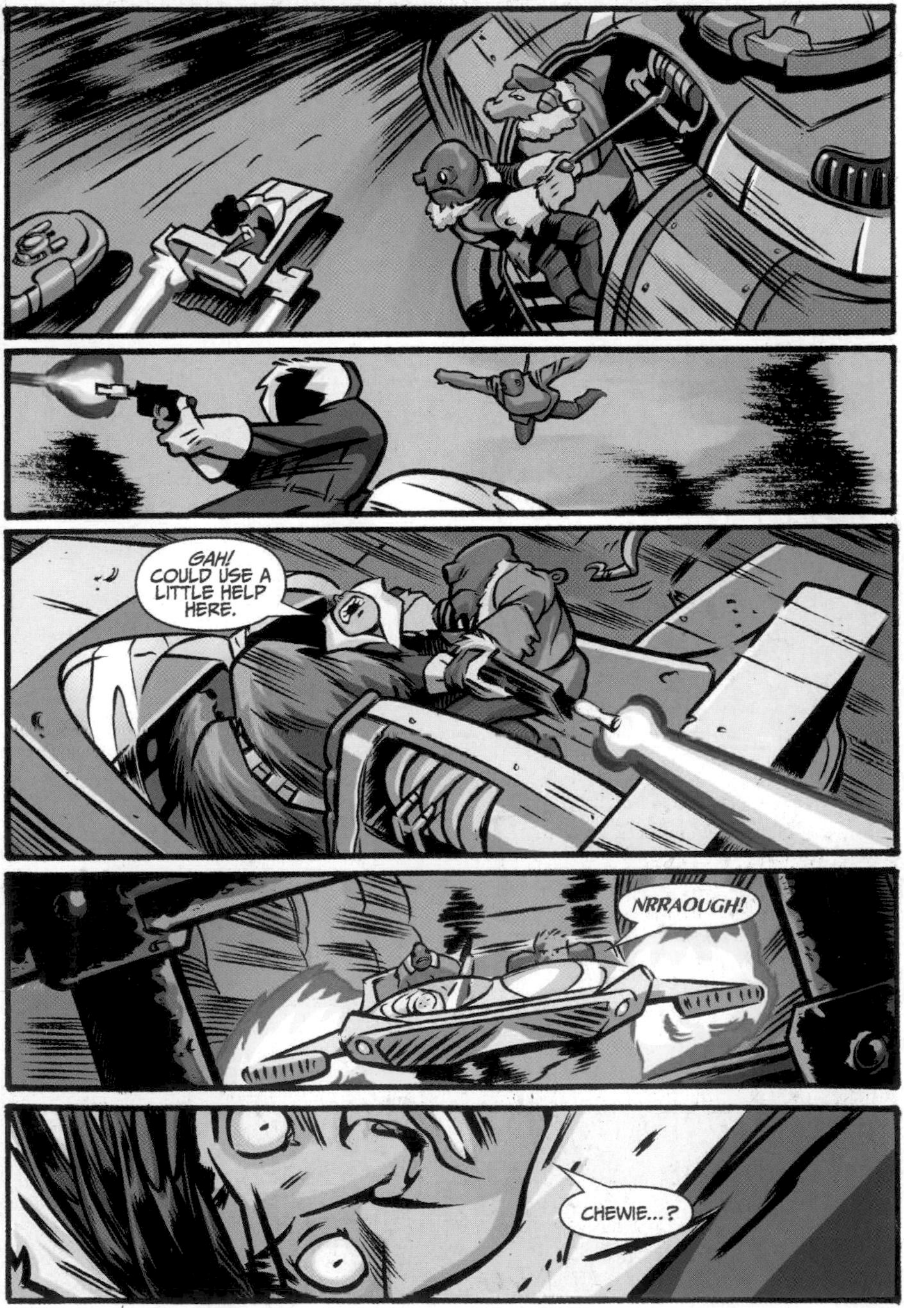
GAH! COULD USE A LITTLE HELP HERE.
NRRAOUGH!
CHEWIE...?

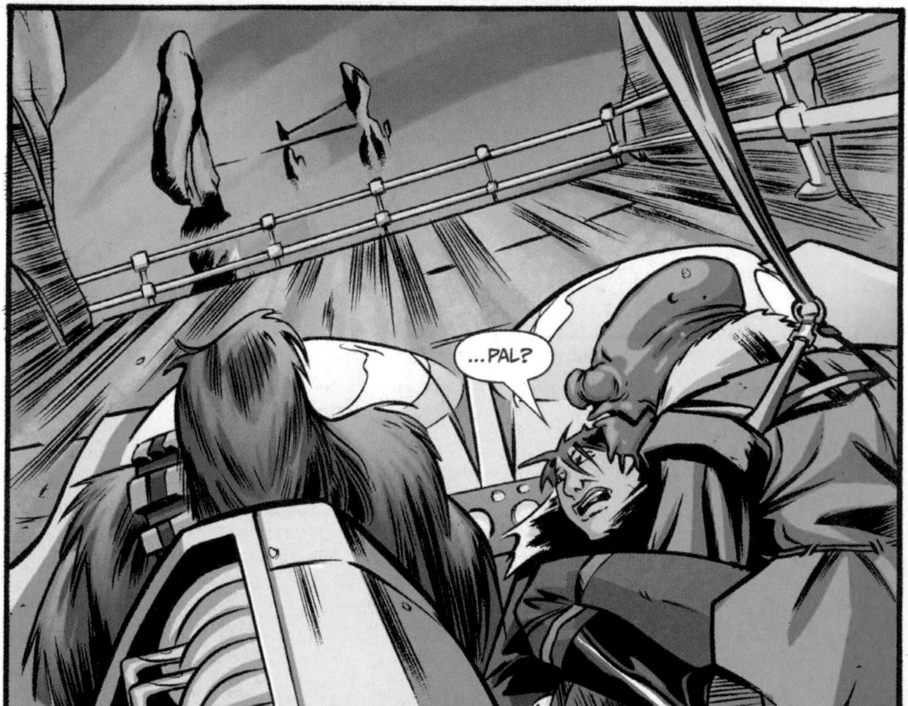
...PAL?
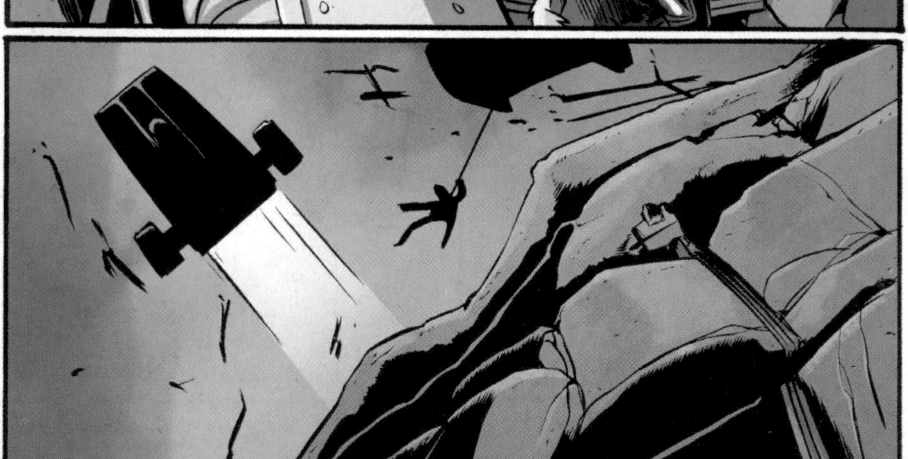

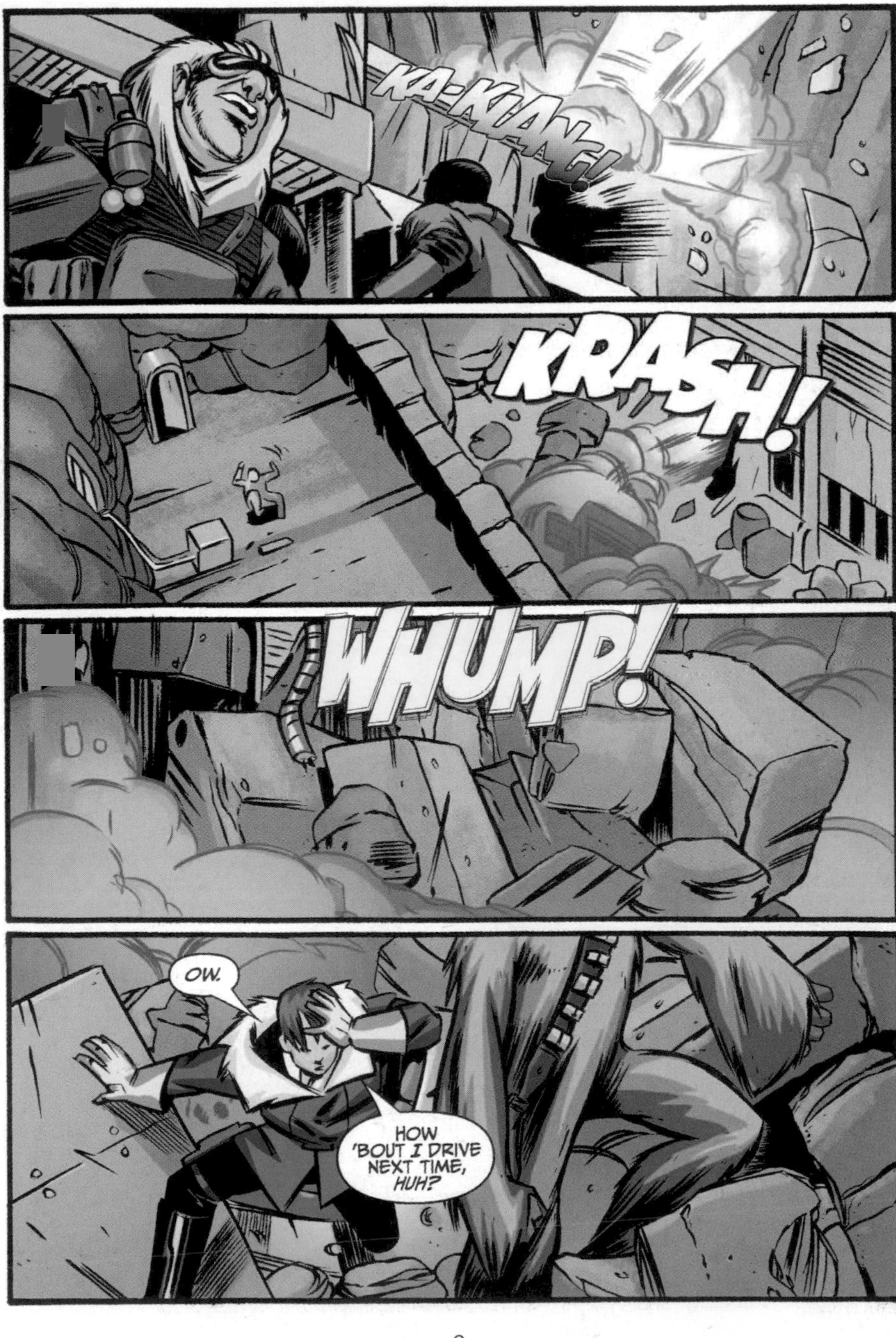
KA-KLANG!
KRASH!
WHUMP!
OW.
HOW 'BOUT I DRIVE NEXT TIME, HUH?

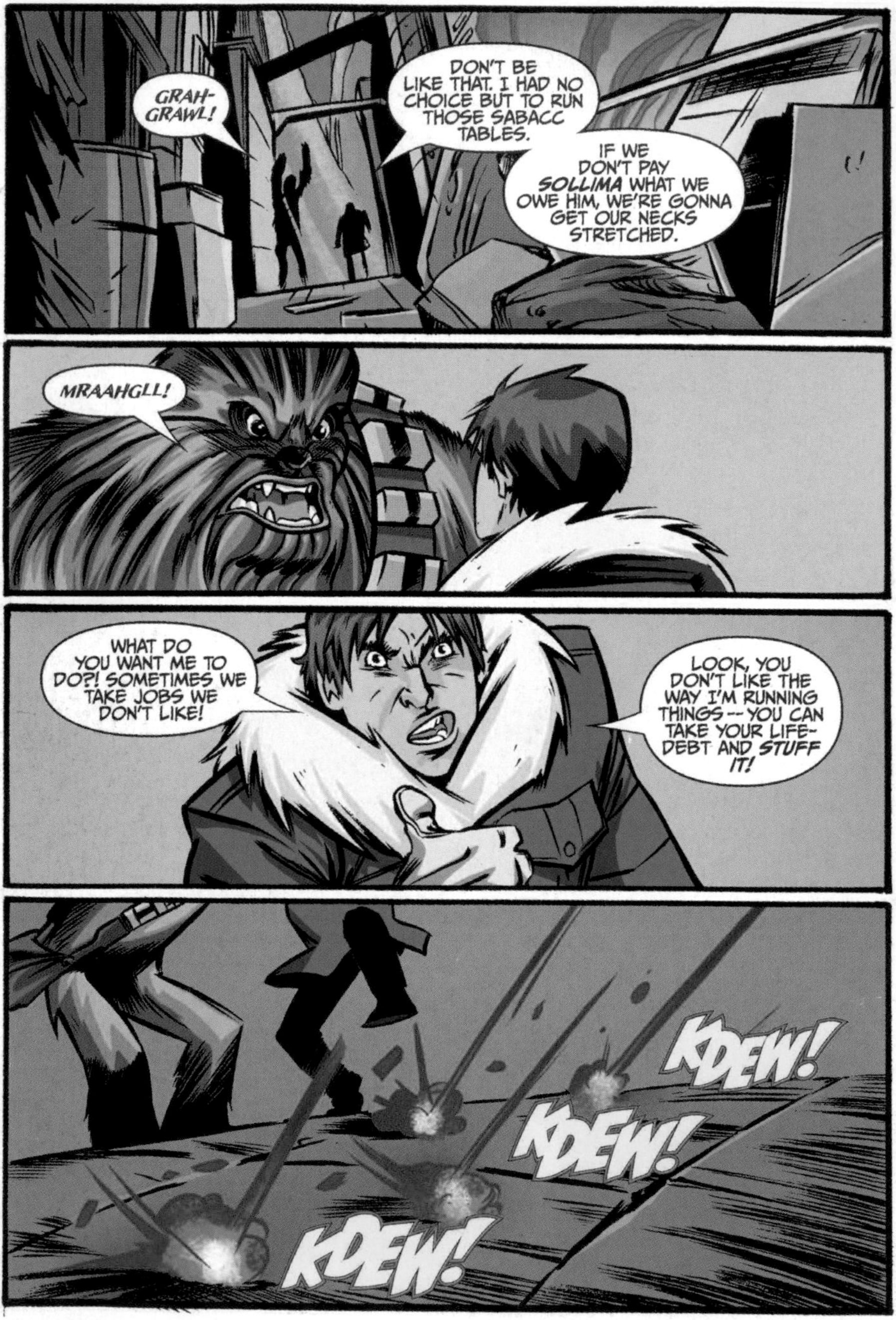
GRAH-GRAWL!
DON'T BE LIKE THAT. I HAD NO CHOICE BUT TO RUN THOSE SABACC TABLES.
IF WE DON'T PAY SOLLIMA WHAT WE OWE HIM, WE'RE GONNA GET OUR NECKS STRETCHED.
MRAAHGLL!
WHAT DO YOU WANT ME TO DO?! SOMETIMES WE TAKE JOBS WE DON'T LIKE!
LOOK, YOU DON'T LIKE THE WAY I'M RUNNING THINGS-- YOU CAN TAKE YOUR LIFE-DEBT AND STUFF IT!
KDEW!
KDEW!
KDEW!

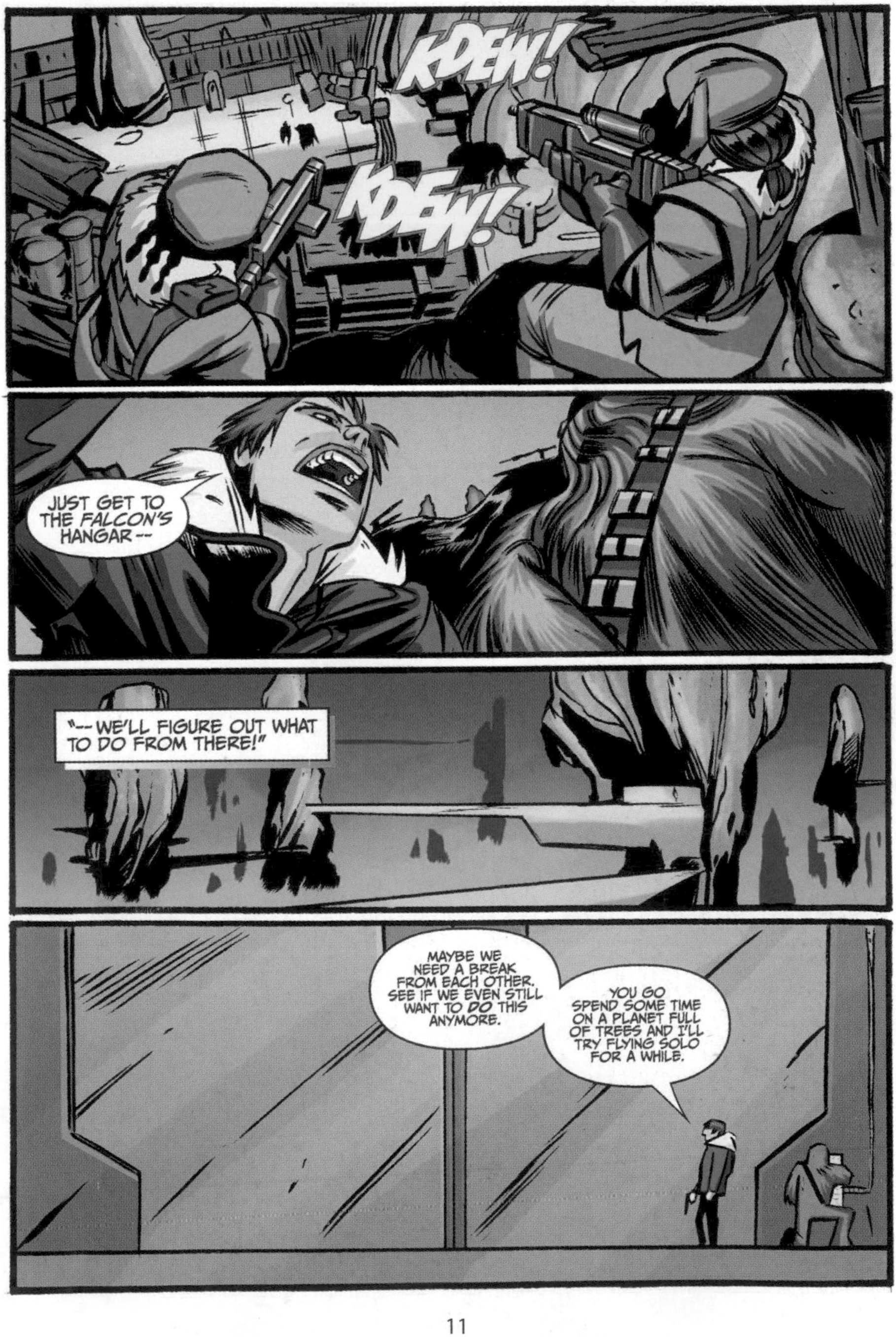
KDEW!
KDEW!
JUST GET TO THE FALCON'S HANGAR--
"--WE'LL FIGURE OUT WHAT TO DO FROM THERE!"
MAYBE WE NEED A BREAK FROM EACH OTHER. SEE IF WE EVEN STILL WANT TO DO THIS ANYMORE.
YOU GO SPEND SOME TIME ON A PLANET FULL OF TREES AND I'LL TRY FLYING SOLO FOR A WHILE.

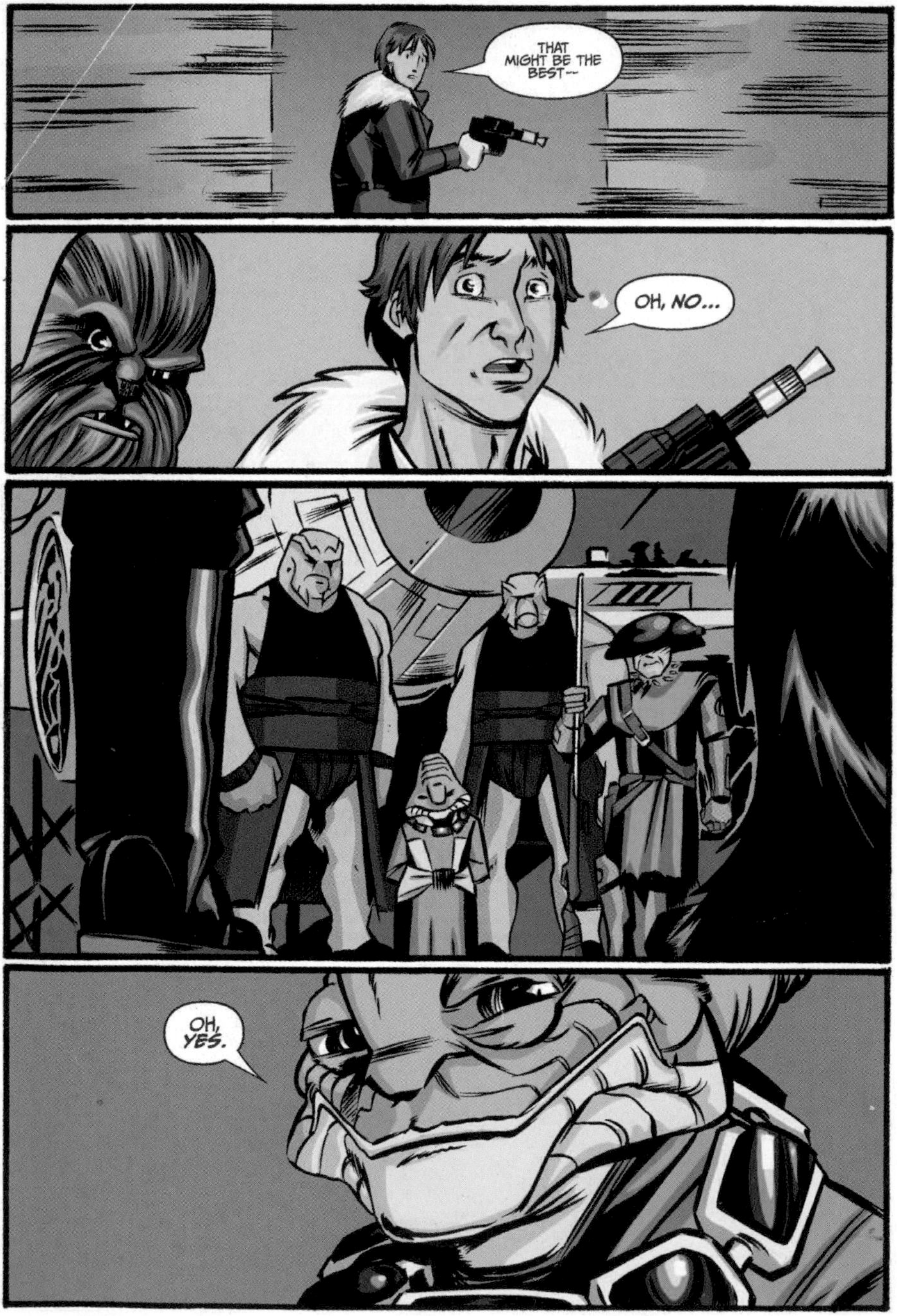
THAT MIGHT BE THE BEST--
OH, NO...
OH, YES.

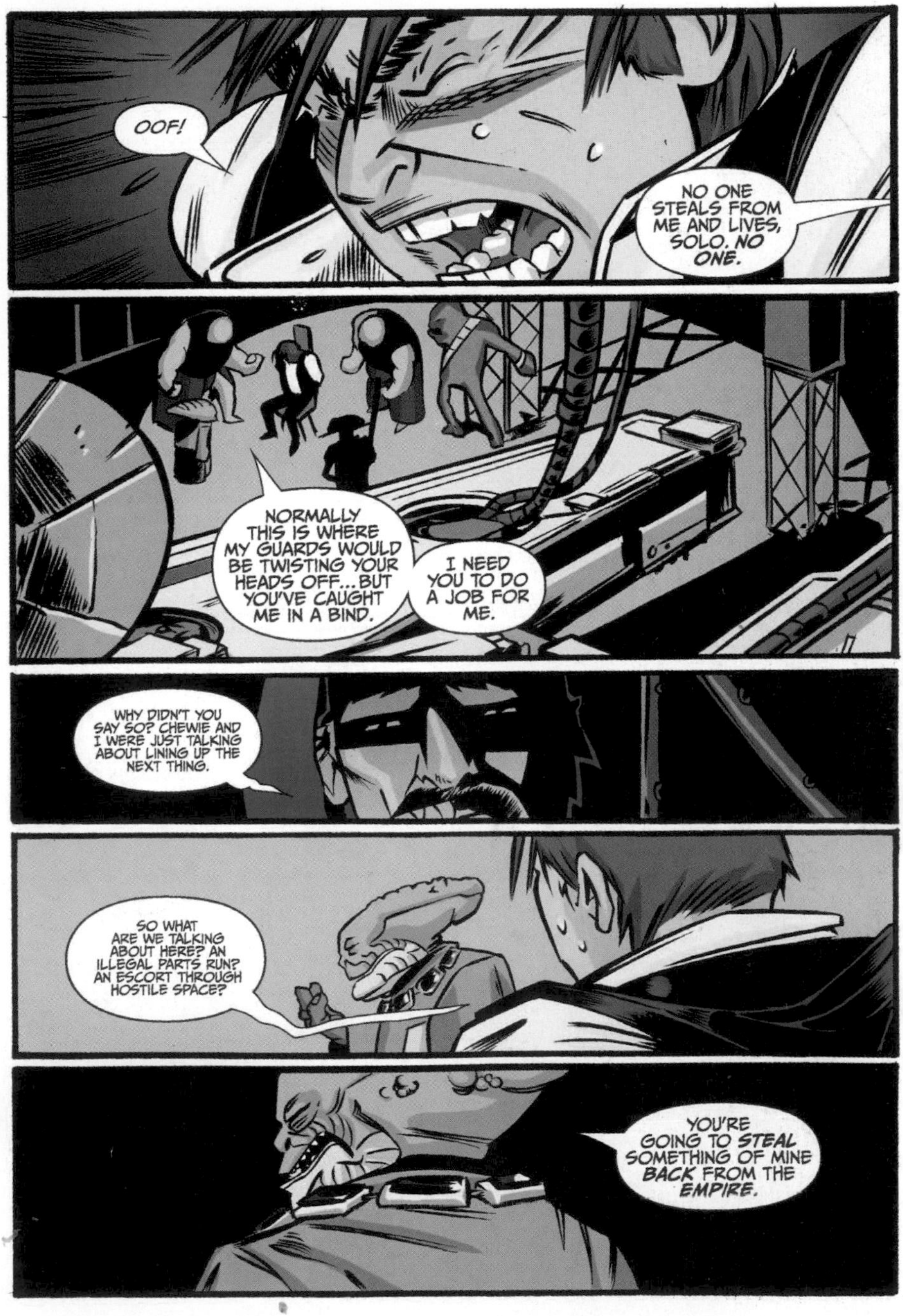
OOF!
NO ONE STEALS FROM ME AND LIVES, SOLO. NO ONE.
NORMALLY THIS IS WHERE MY GUARDS WOULD BE TWISTING YOUR HEADS OFF... BUT YOU'VE CAUGHT ME IN A BIND.
I NEED YOU TO DO A JOB FOR ME.
WHY DIDN'T YOU SAY SO? CHEWIE AND I WERE JUST TALKING ABOUT LINING UP THE NEXT THING.
SO WHAT ARE WE TALKING ABOUT HERE? AN ILLEGAL PARTS RUN? AN ESCORT THROUGH HOSTILE SPACE?
YOU'RE GOING TO STEAL SOMETHING OF MINE BACK FROM THE EMPIRE.

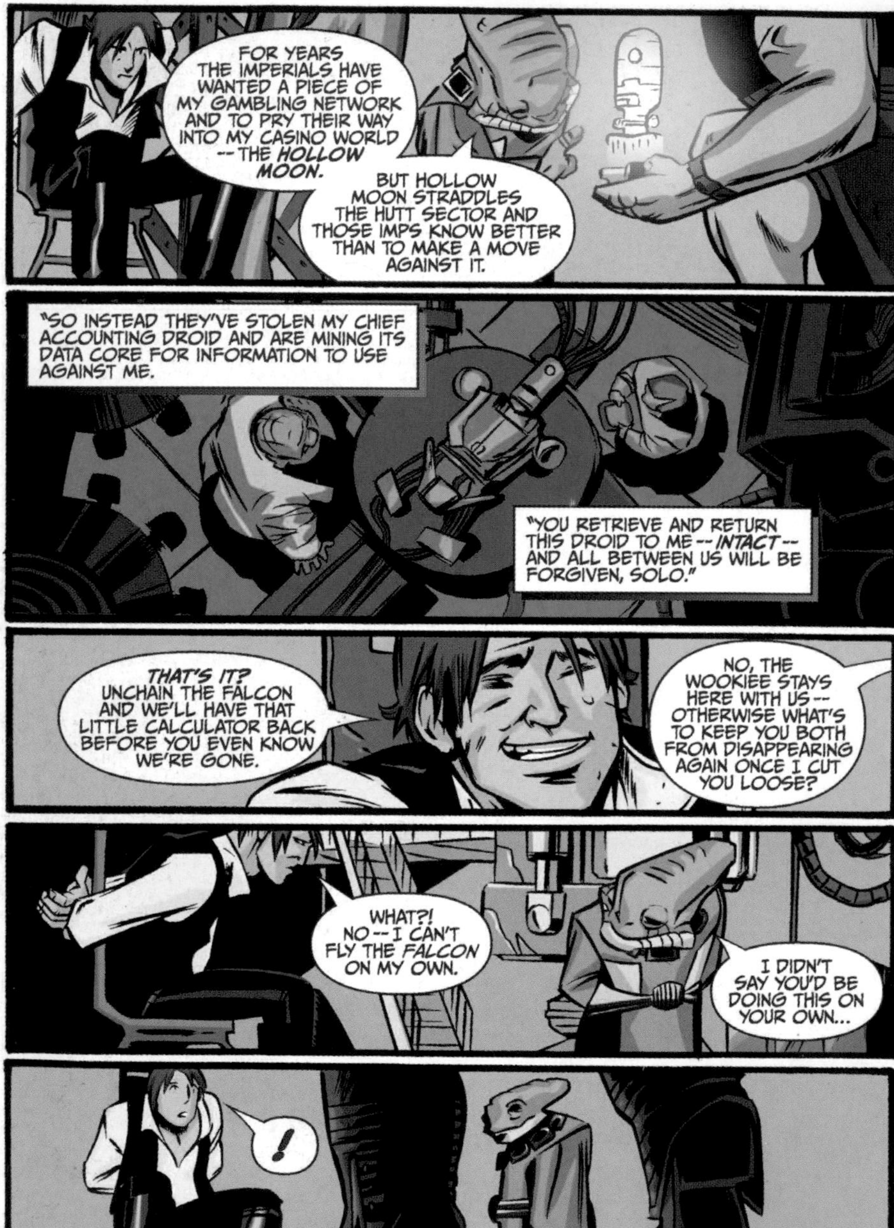

FOR YEARS THE IMPERIALS HAVE WANTED A PIECE OF MY GAMBLING NETWORK AND TO PRY THEIR WAY INTO MY CASINO WORLD --THE *HOLLOW MOON.*
BUT HOLLOW MOON STRADDLES THE HUTT SECTOR AND THOSE IMPS KNOW BETTER THAN TO MAKE A MOVE AGAINST IT.
"SO INSTEAD THEY'VE STOLEN MY CHIEF ACCOUNTING DROID AND ARE MINING ITS DATA CORE FOR INFORMATION TO USE AGAINST ME.
"YOU RETRIEVE AND RETURN THIS DROID TO ME--*INTACT*-- AND ALL BETWEEN US WILL BE FORGIVEN, SOLO."
THAT'S IT? UNCHAIN THE FALCON AND WE'LL HAVE THAT LITTLE CALCULATOR BACK BEFORE YOU EVEN KNOW WE'RE GONE.
NO, THE WOOKIEE STAYS HERE WITH US-- OTHERWISE WHAT'S TO KEEP YOU BOTH FROM DISAPPEARING AGAIN ONCE I CUT YOU LOOSE?
WHAT?! NO--I CAN'T FLY THE *FALCON* ON MY OWN.
I DIDN'T SAY YOU'D BE DOING THIS ON YOUR OWN...
!

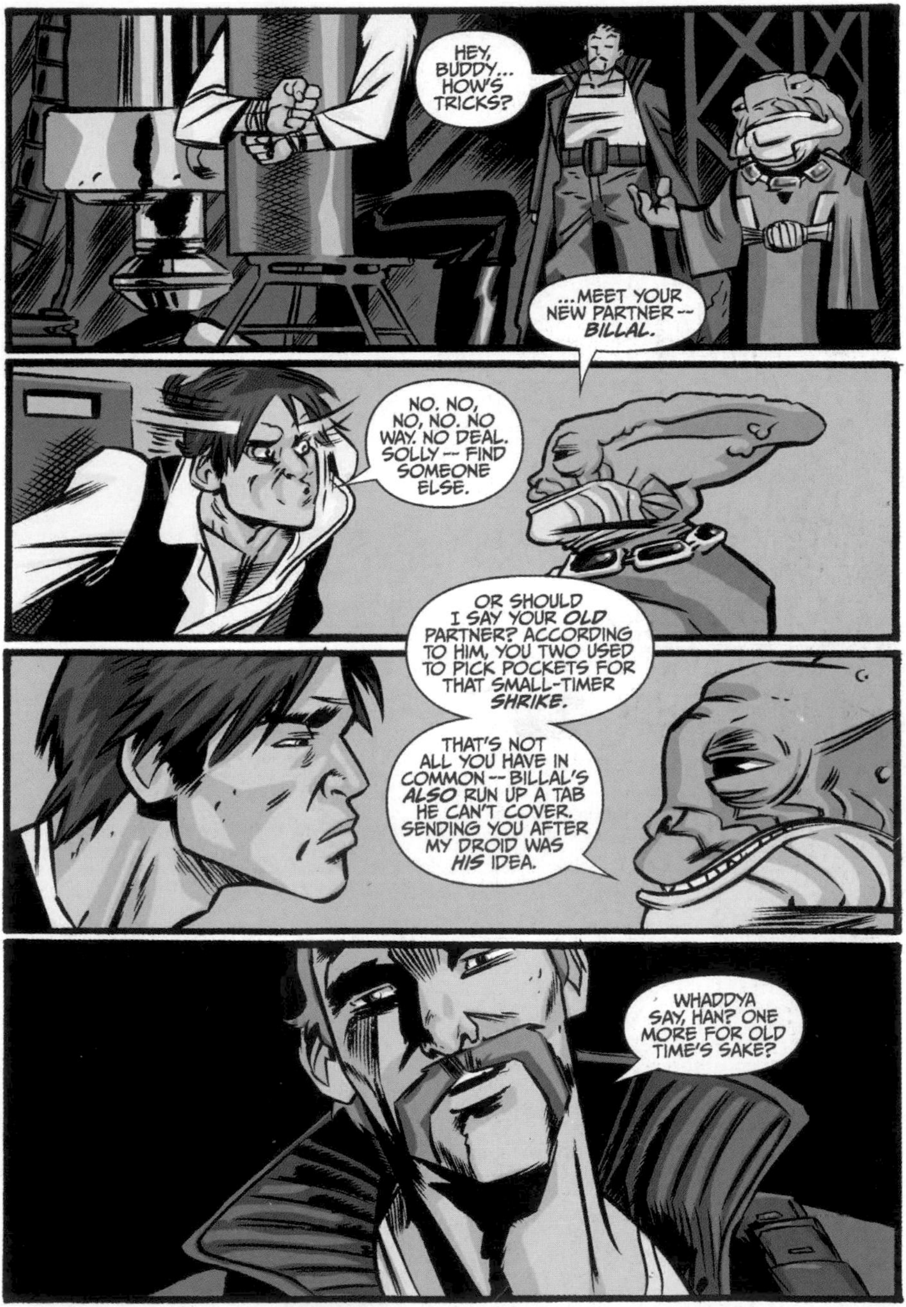
HEY, BUDDY... HOW'S TRICKS?
...MEET YOUR NEW PARTNER -- BILLAL.
NO. NO, NO, NO. NO WAY. NO DEAL. SOLLY -- FIND SOMEONE ELSE.
OR SHOULD I SAY YOUR OLD PARTNER? ACCORDING TO HIM, YOU TWO USED TO PICK POCKETS FOR THAT SMALL-TIMER SHRIKE.
THAT'S NOT ALL YOU HAVE IN COMMON -- BILLAL'S ALSO RUN UP A TAB HE CAN'T COVER. SENDING YOU AFTER MY DROID WAS HIS IDEA.
WHADDYA SAY, HAN? ONE MORE FOR OLD TIME'S SAKE?

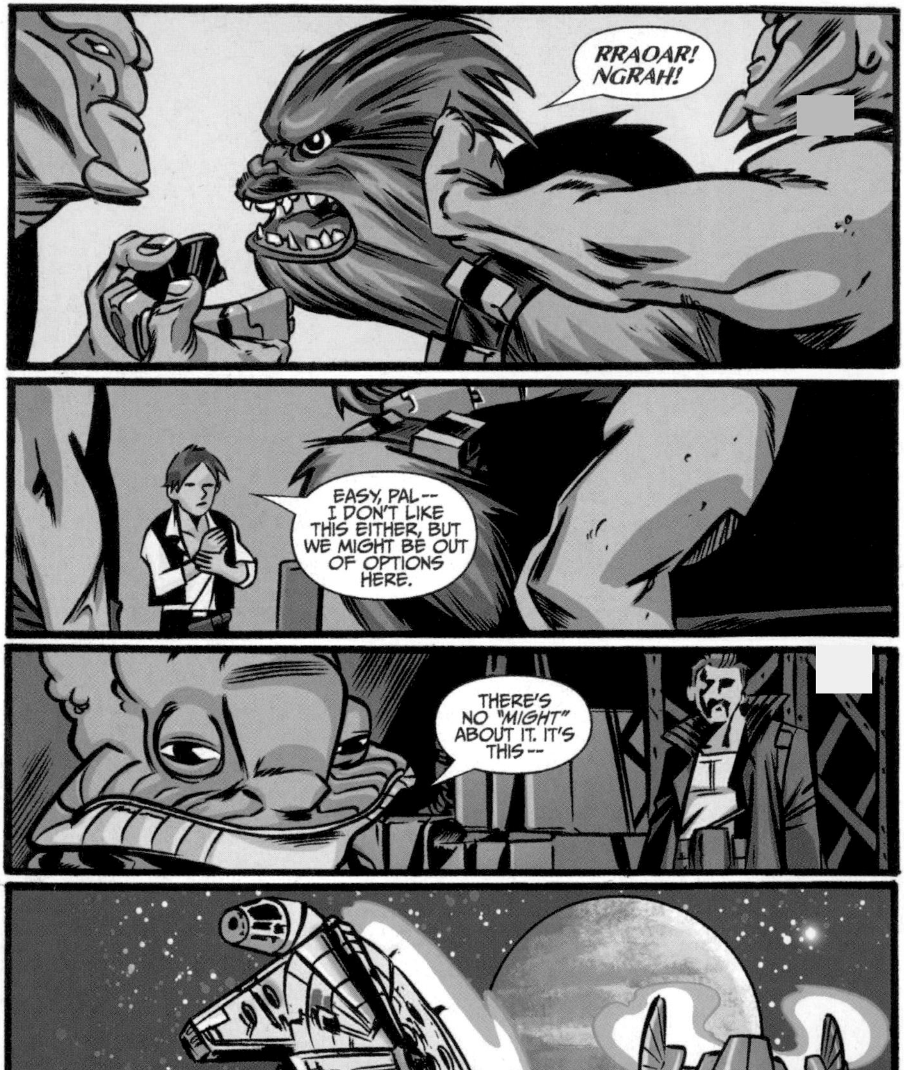
RRAOAR! NGRAH!
EASY, PAL -- I DON'T LIKE THIS EITHER, BUT WE MIGHT BE OUT OF OPTIONS HERE.
THERE'S NO "MIGHT" ABOUT IT. IT'S THIS --
"-- OR I PUT YOUR BONES INTO THE FOUNDATION OF MY NEXT CASINO."

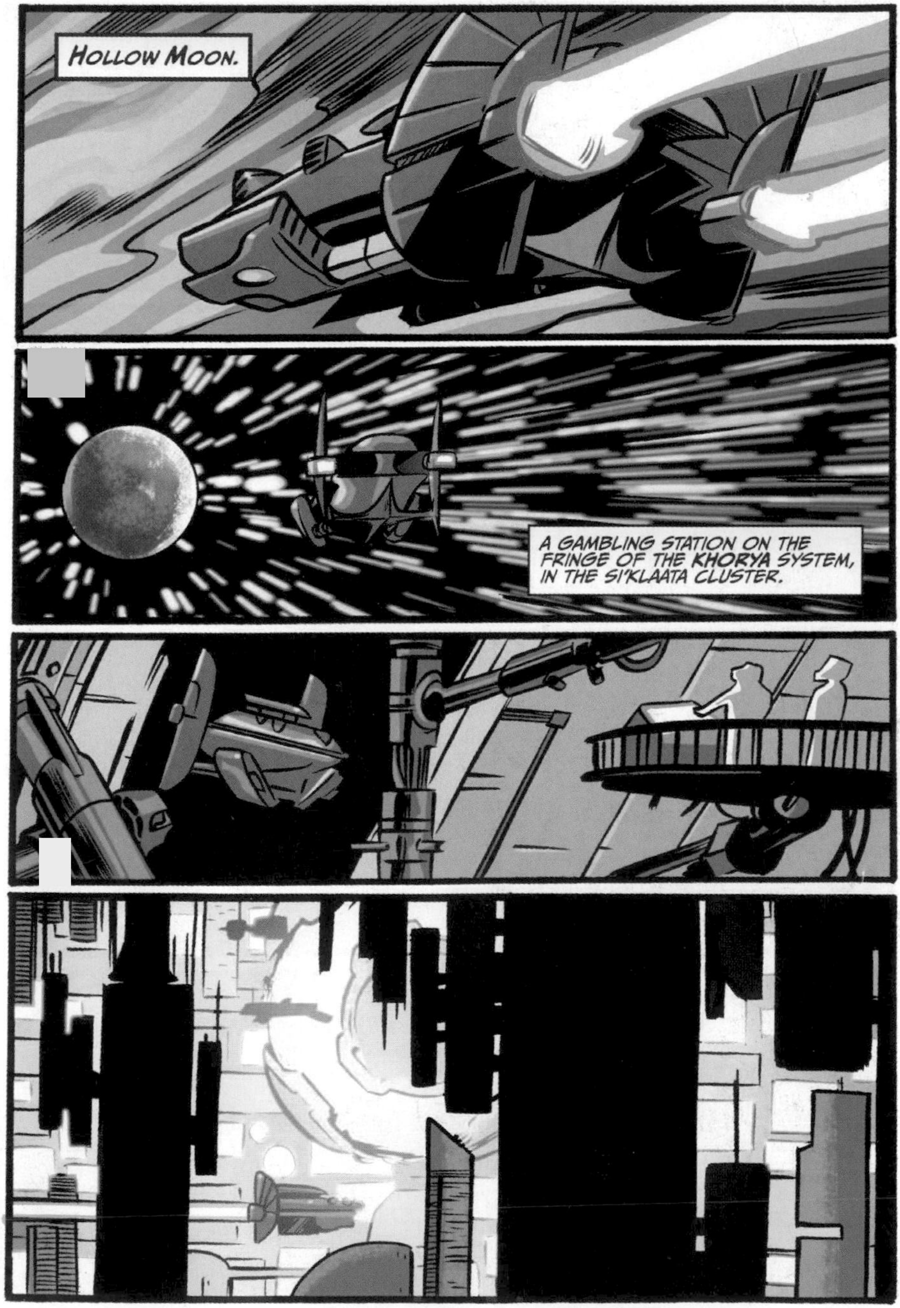
HOLLOW MOON.
A GAMBLING STATION ON THE FRINGE OF THE KHORYA SYSTEM, IN THE SI'KLAATA CLUSTER.

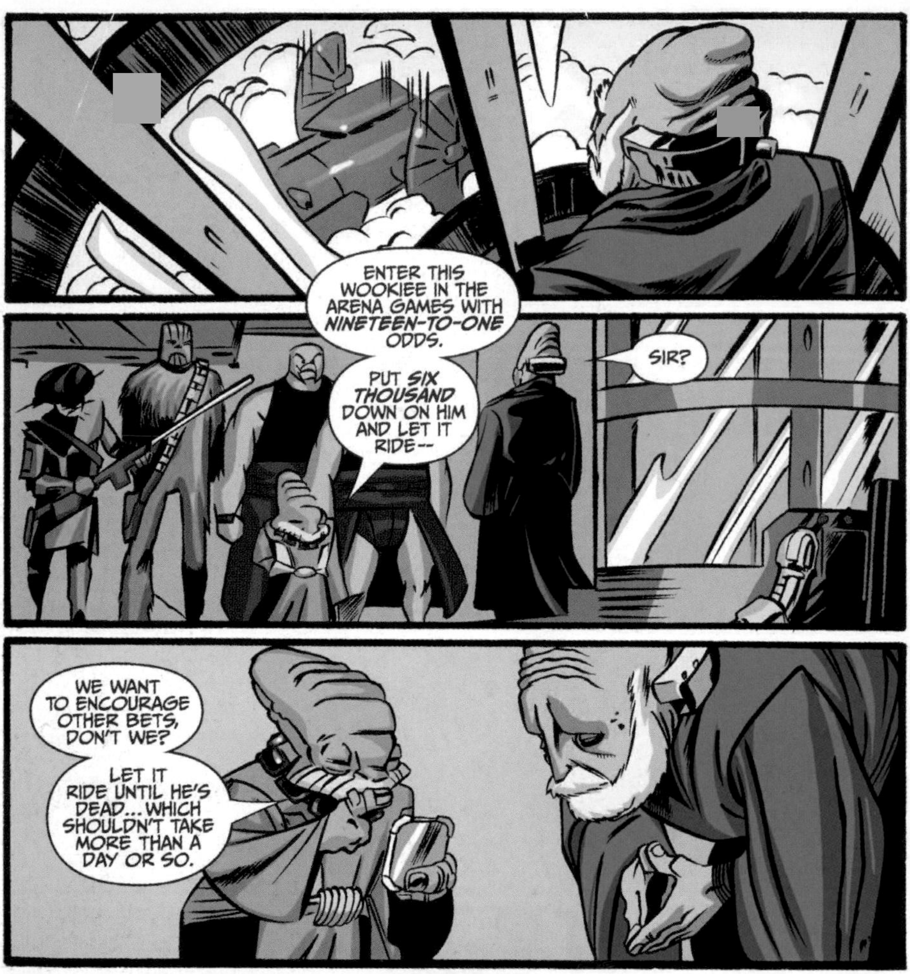
ENTER THIS WOOKIEE IN THE ARENA GAMES WITH *NINETEEN-TO-ONE* ODDS.
PUT *SIX THOUSAND* DOWN ON HIM AND LET IT RIDE--
SIR?
WE WANT TO ENCOURAGE OTHER BETS, DON'T WE?
LET IT RIDE UNTIL HE'S DEAD... WHICH SHOULDN'T TAKE MORE THAN A DAY OR SO.
JUST MAKE SURE HE'S A *MEMORY* BEFORE SOLO RETURNS WITH MY DROID.

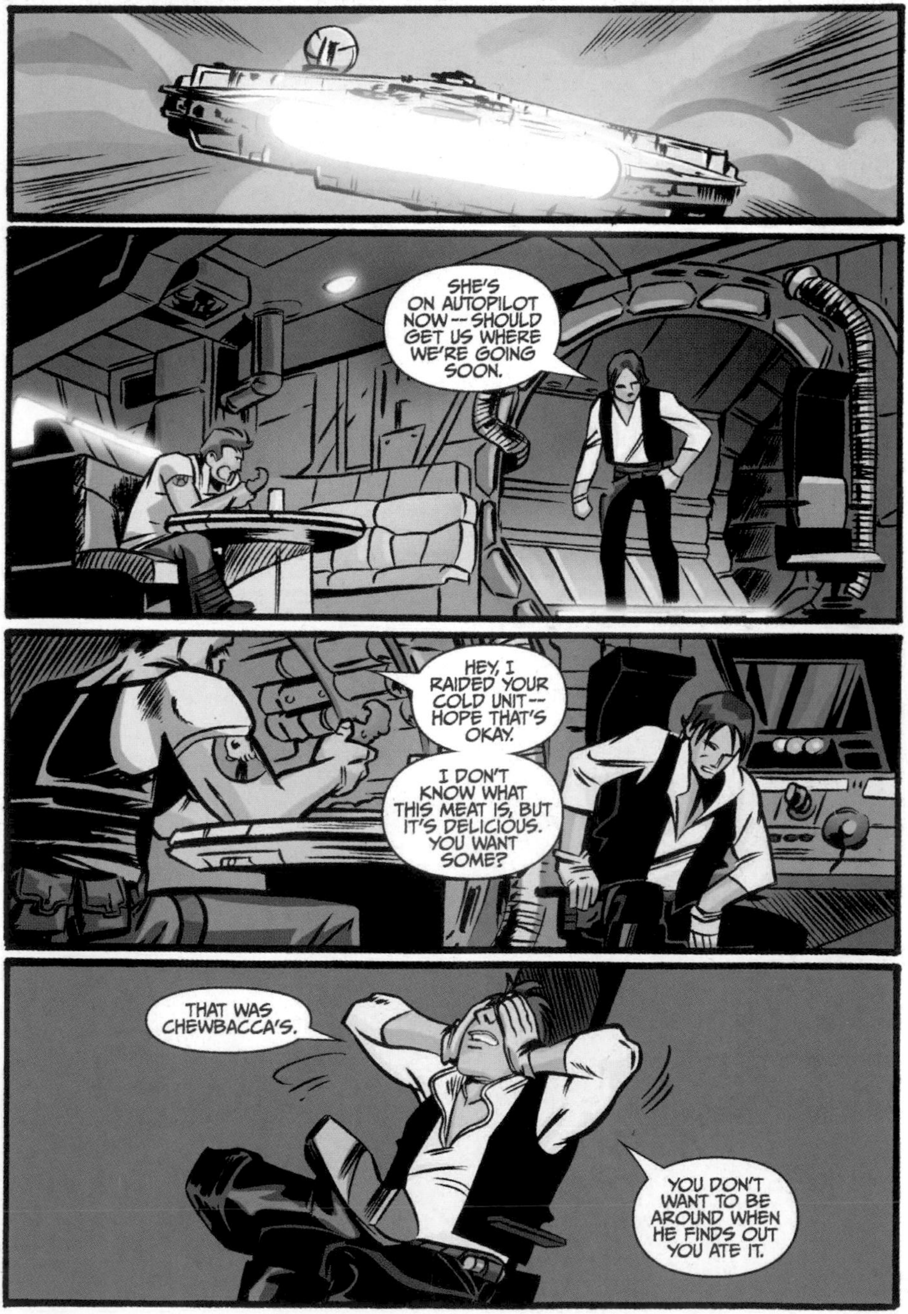
SHE'S ON AUTOPILOT NOW--SHOULD GET US WHERE WE'RE GOING SOON.
HEY, I RAIDED YOUR COLD UNIT--HOPE THAT'S OKAY.
I DON'T KNOW WHAT THIS MEAT IS, BUT IT'S DELICIOUS. YOU WANT SOME?
THAT WAS CHEWBACCA'S.
YOU DON'T WANT TO BE AROUND WHEN HE FINDS OUT YOU ATE IT.

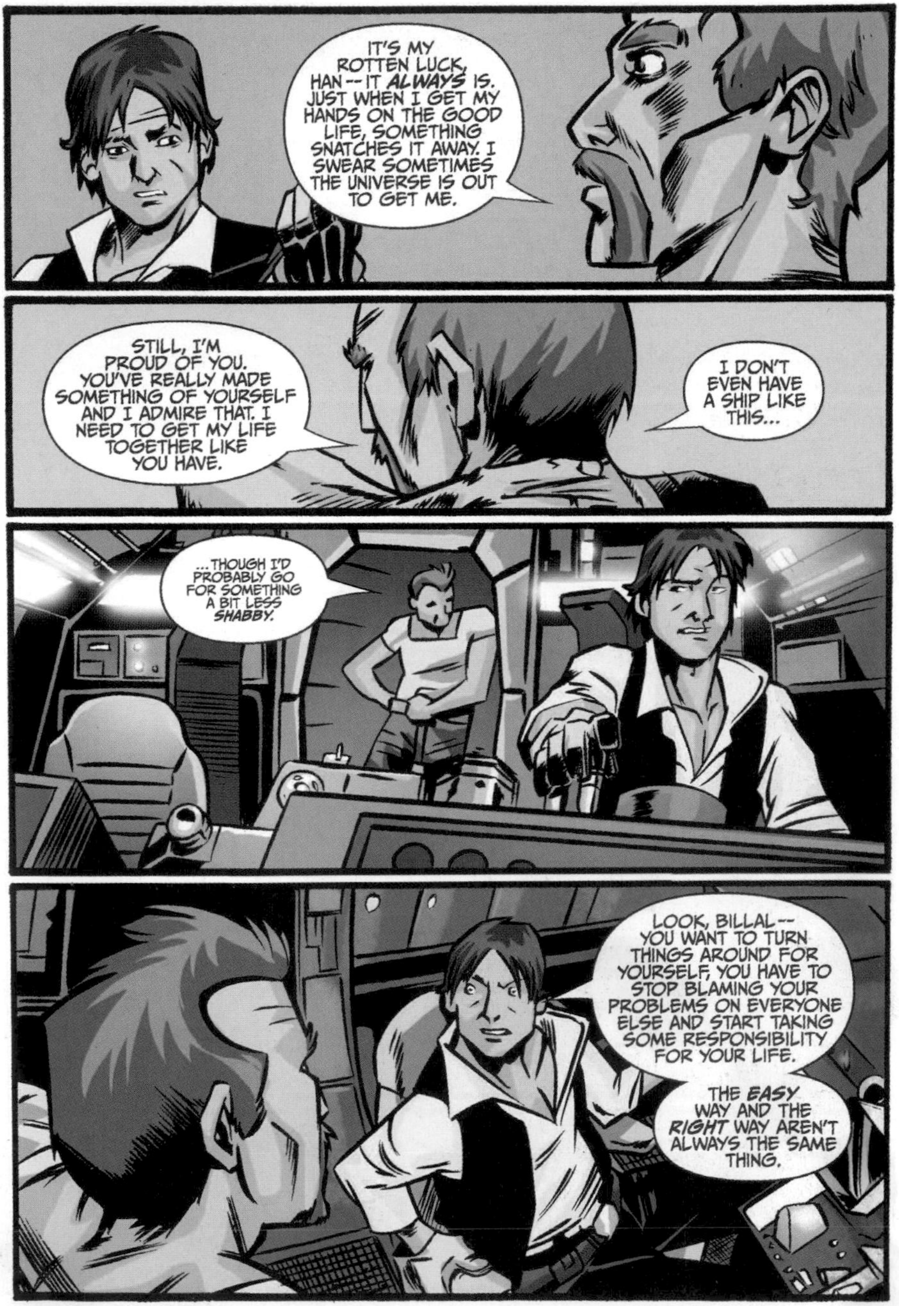
IT'S MY ROTTEN LUCK, HAN -- IT ALWAYS IS. JUST WHEN I GET MY HANDS ON THE GOOD LIFE, SOMETHING SNATCHES IT AWAY. I SWEAR SOMETIMES THE UNIVERSE IS OUT TO GET ME.
STILL, I'M PROUD OF YOU. YOU'VE REALLY MADE SOMETHING OF YOURSELF AND I ADMIRE THAT. I NEED TO GET MY LIFE TOGETHER LIKE YOU HAVE.
I DON'T EVEN HAVE A SHIP LIKE THIS...
...THOUGH I'D PROBABLY GO FOR SOMETHING A BIT LESS SHABBY.
LOOK, BILLAL -- YOU WANT TO TURN THINGS AROUND FOR YOURSELF, YOU HAVE TO STOP BLAMING YOUR PROBLEMS ON EVERYONE ELSE AND START TAKING SOME RESPONSIBILITY FOR YOUR LIFE.
THE EASY WAY AND THE RIGHT WAY AREN'T ALWAYS THE SAME THING.

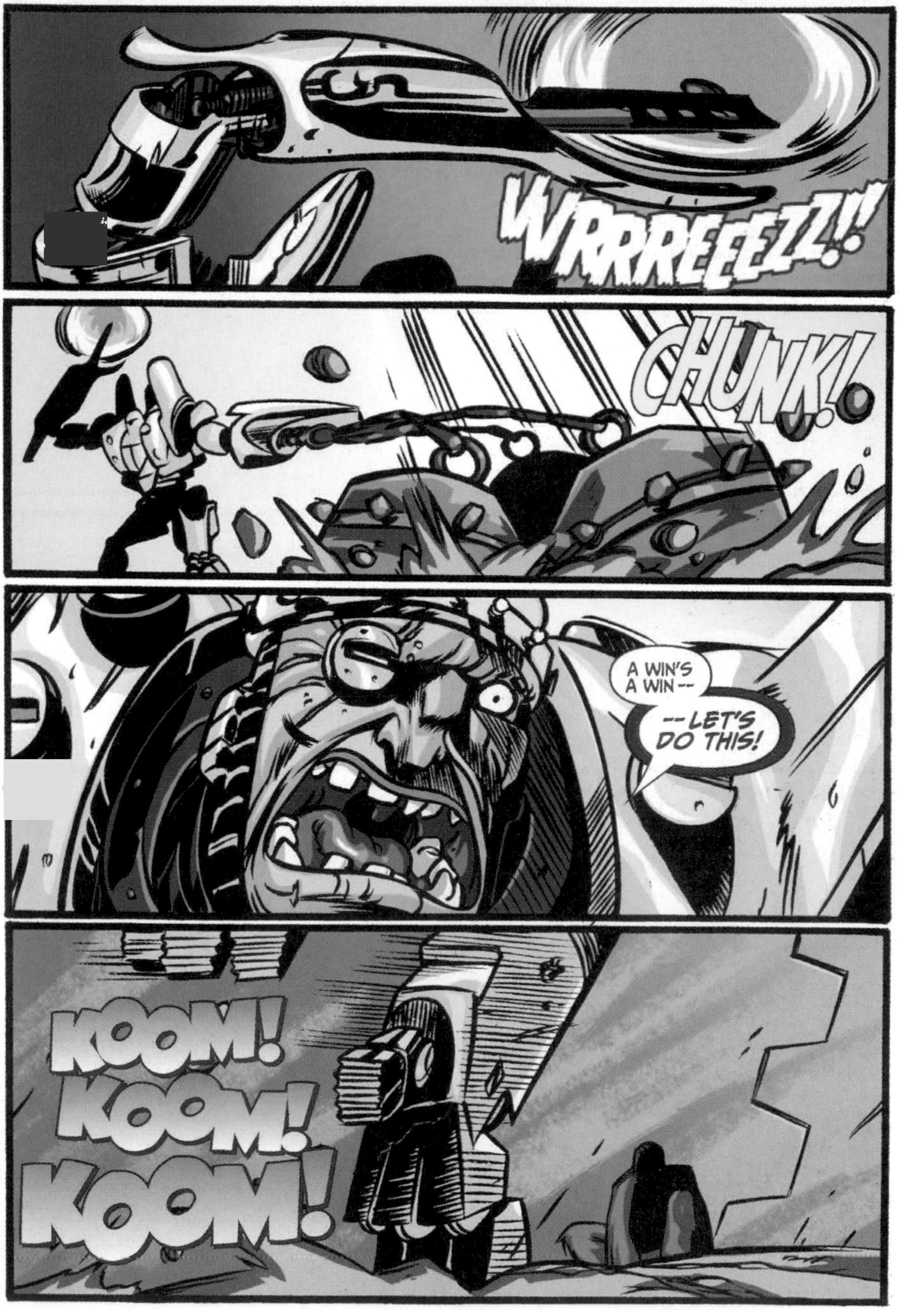
WRRREEEZZ!!
CHUNK!
A WIN'S A WIN --
-- LET'S DO THIS!
KOOM! KOOM! KOOM!

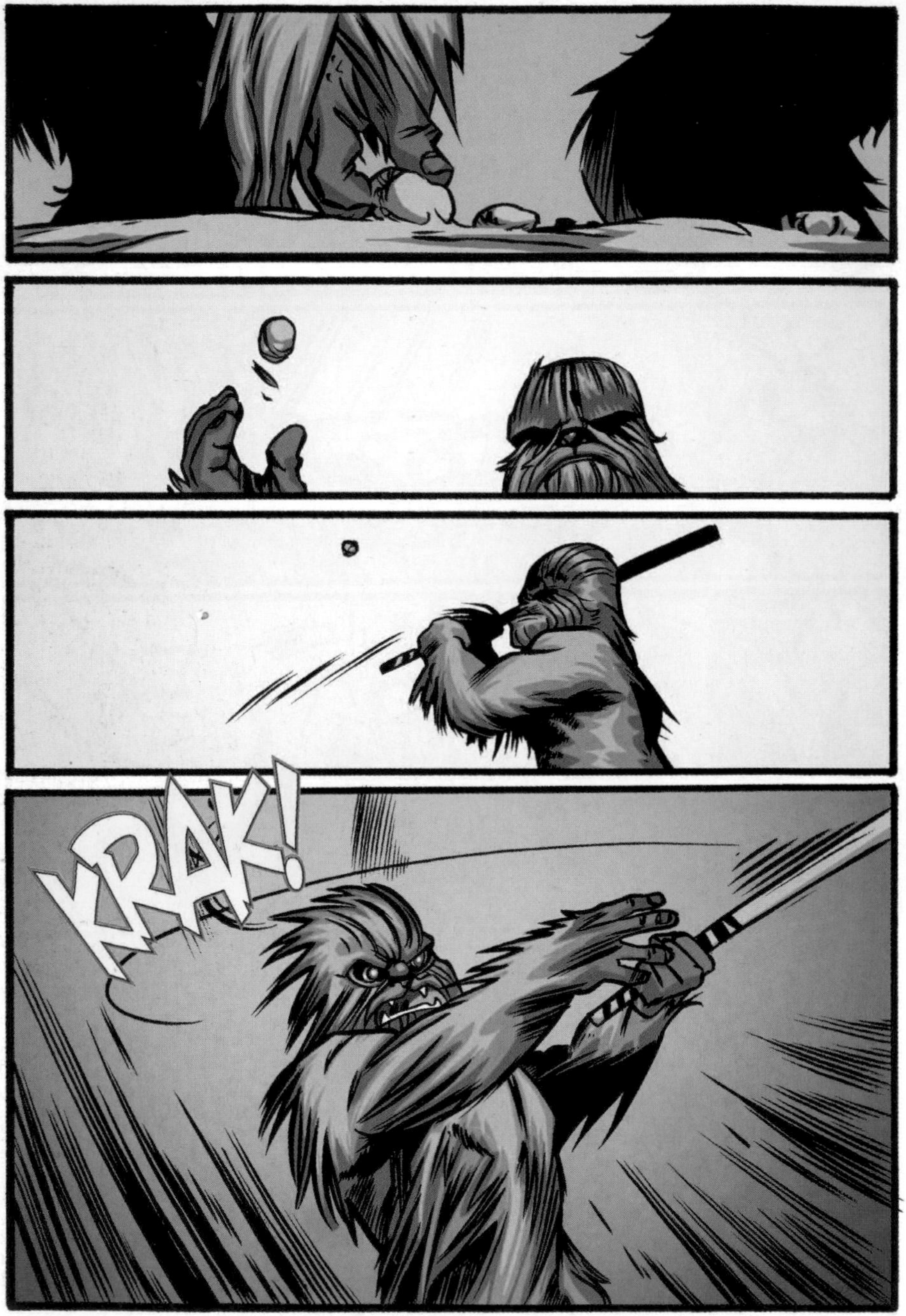
KRAK!

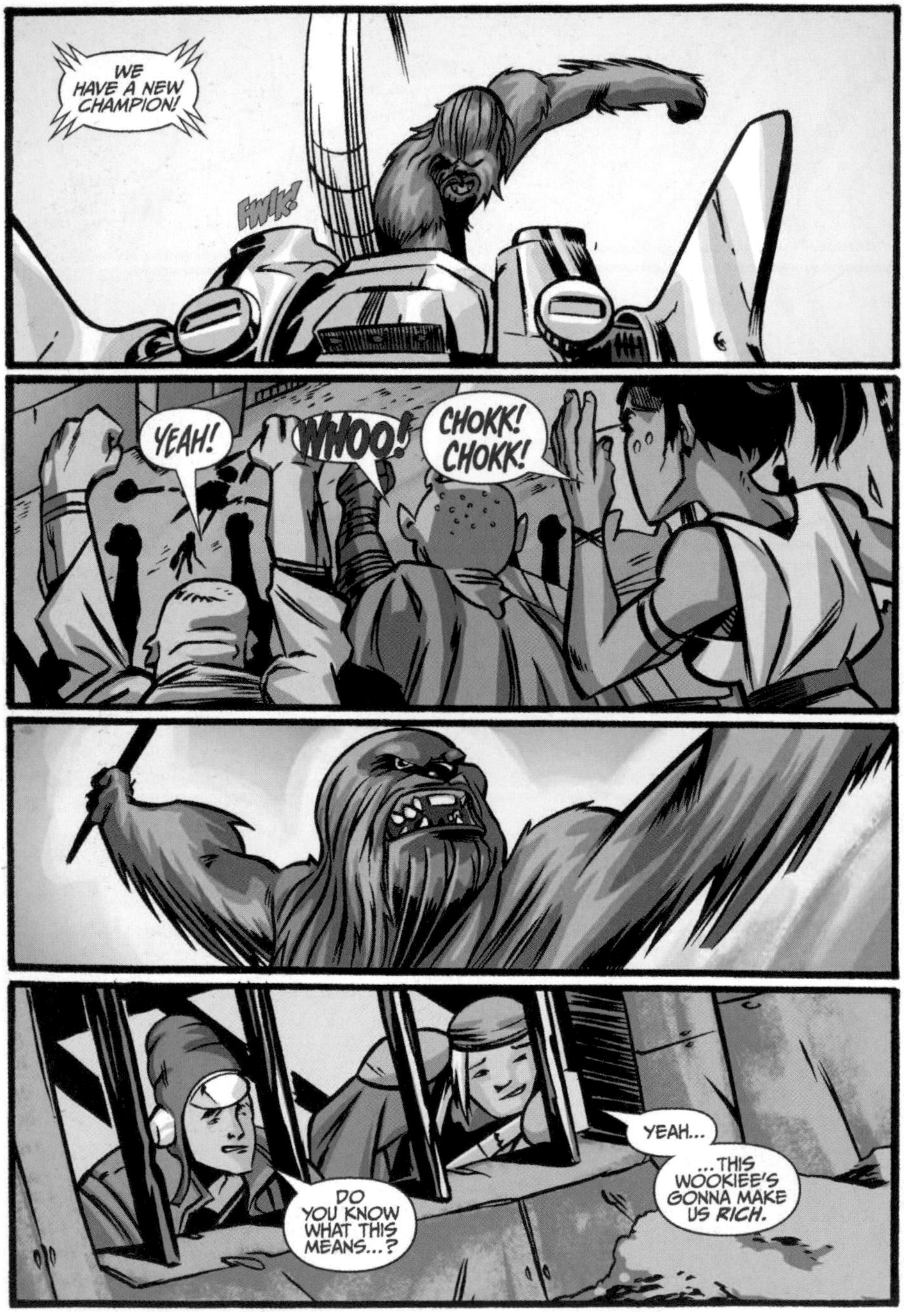
WE HAVE A NEW CHAMPION!
FWIK!
YEAH!
WHOO!
CHOKK! CHOKK!
YEAH...
DO YOU KNOW WHAT THIS MEANS...?
...THIS WOOKIEE'S GONNA MAKE US RICH.

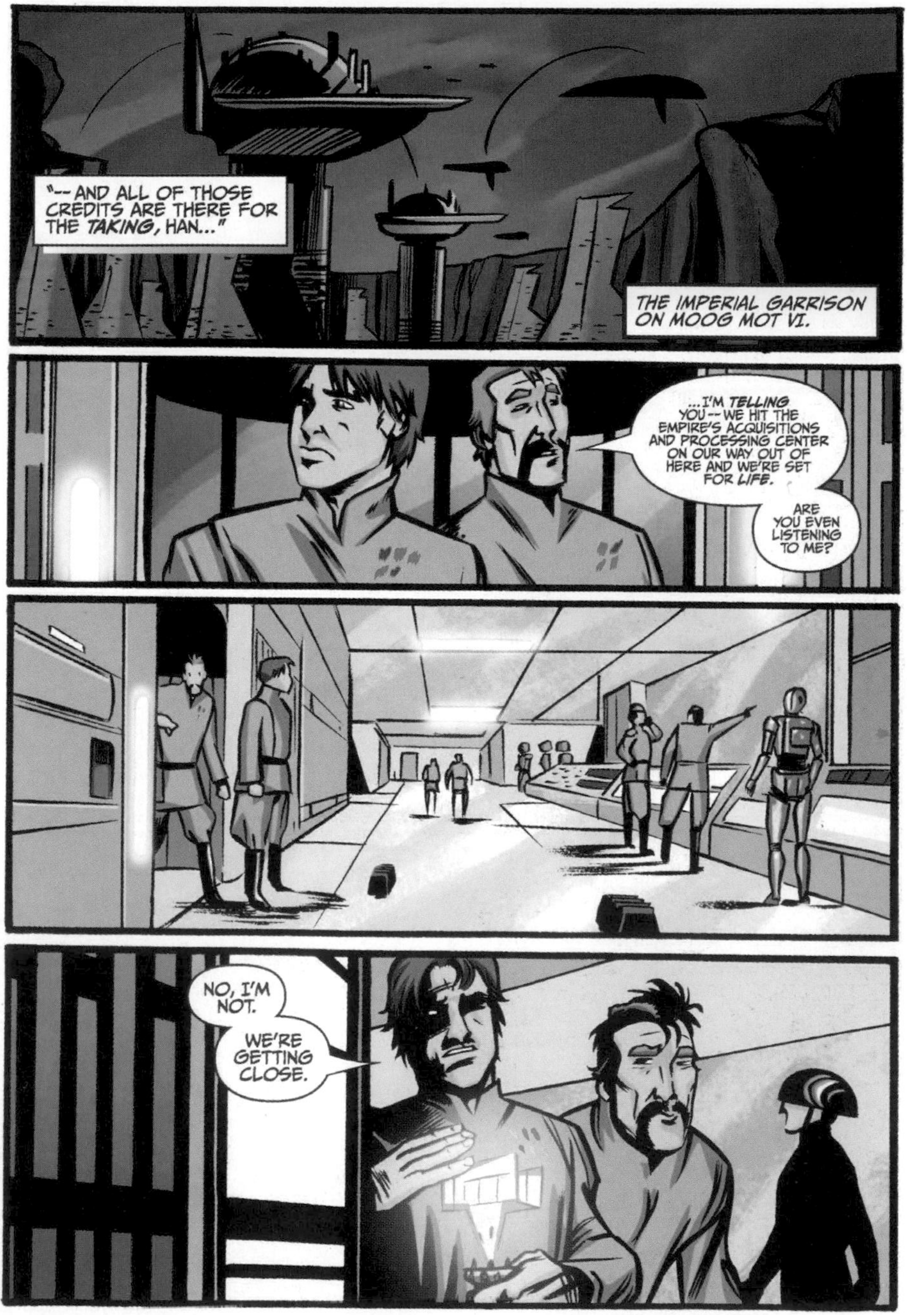
"--AND ALL OF THOSE CREDITS ARE THERE FOR THE TAKING, HAN..."
THE IMPERIAL GARRISON ON MOOG MOT VI.
...I'M TELLING YOU--WE HIT THE EMPIRE'S ACQUISITIONS AND PROCESSING CENTER ON OUR WAY OUT OF HERE AND WE'RE SET FOR LIFE.
ARE YOU EVEN LISTENING TO ME?
NO, I'M NOT.
WE'RE GETTING CLOSE.

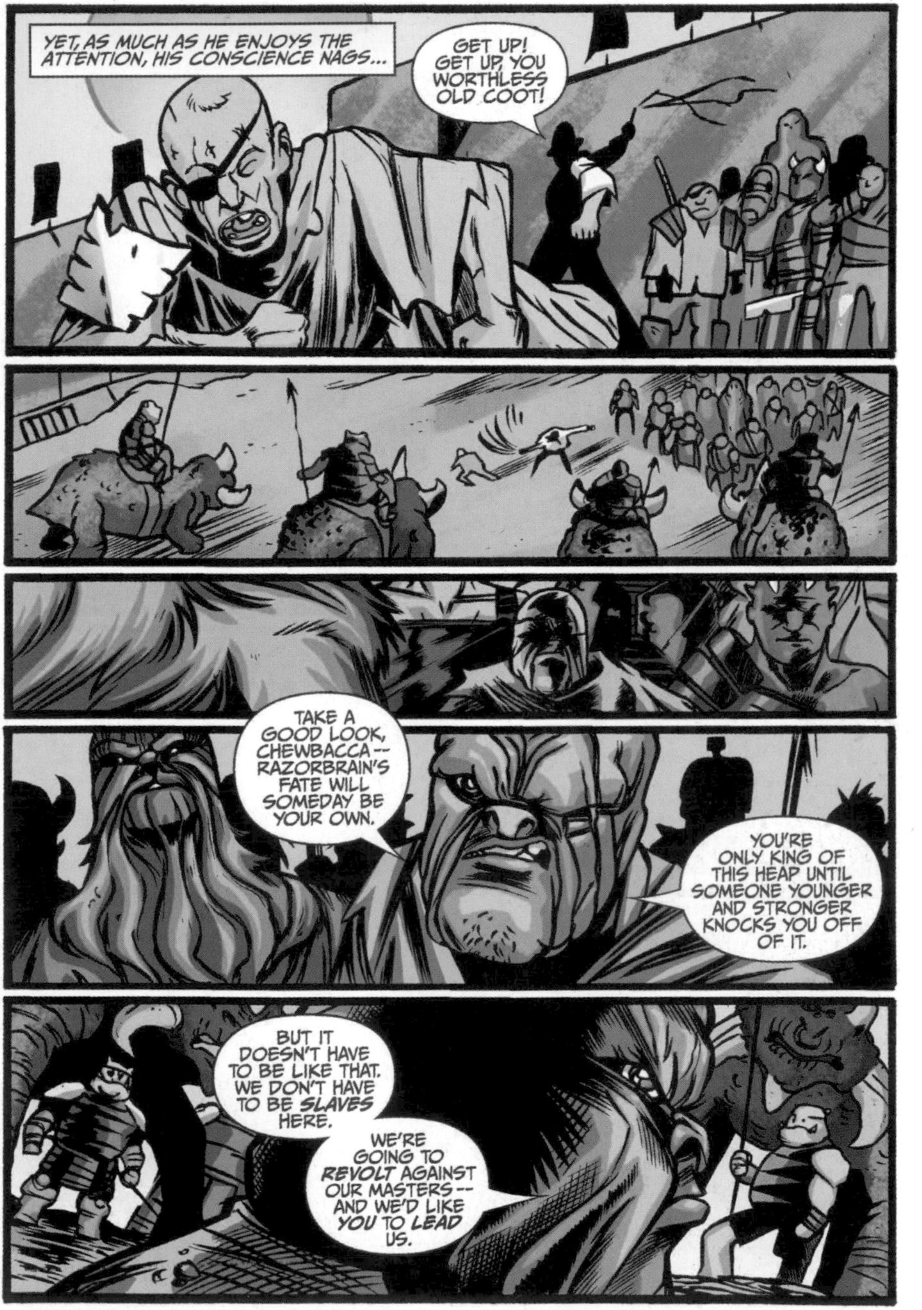
YET, AS MUCH AS HE ENJOYS THE ATTENTION, HIS CONSCIENCE NAGS...
GET UP! GET UP, YOU WORTHLESS OLD COOT!
TAKE A GOOD LOOK, CHEWBACCA -- RAZORBRAIN'S FATE WILL SOMEDAY BE YOUR OWN.
YOU'RE ONLY KING OF THIS HEAP UNTIL SOMEONE YOUNGER AND STRONGER KNOCKS YOU OFF OF IT.
BUT IT DOESN'T HAVE TO BE LIKE THAT. WE DON'T HAVE TO BE *SLAVES* HERE.
WE'RE GOING TO *REVOLT* AGAINST OUR MASTERS -- AND WE'D LIKE *YOU* TO *LEAD* US.

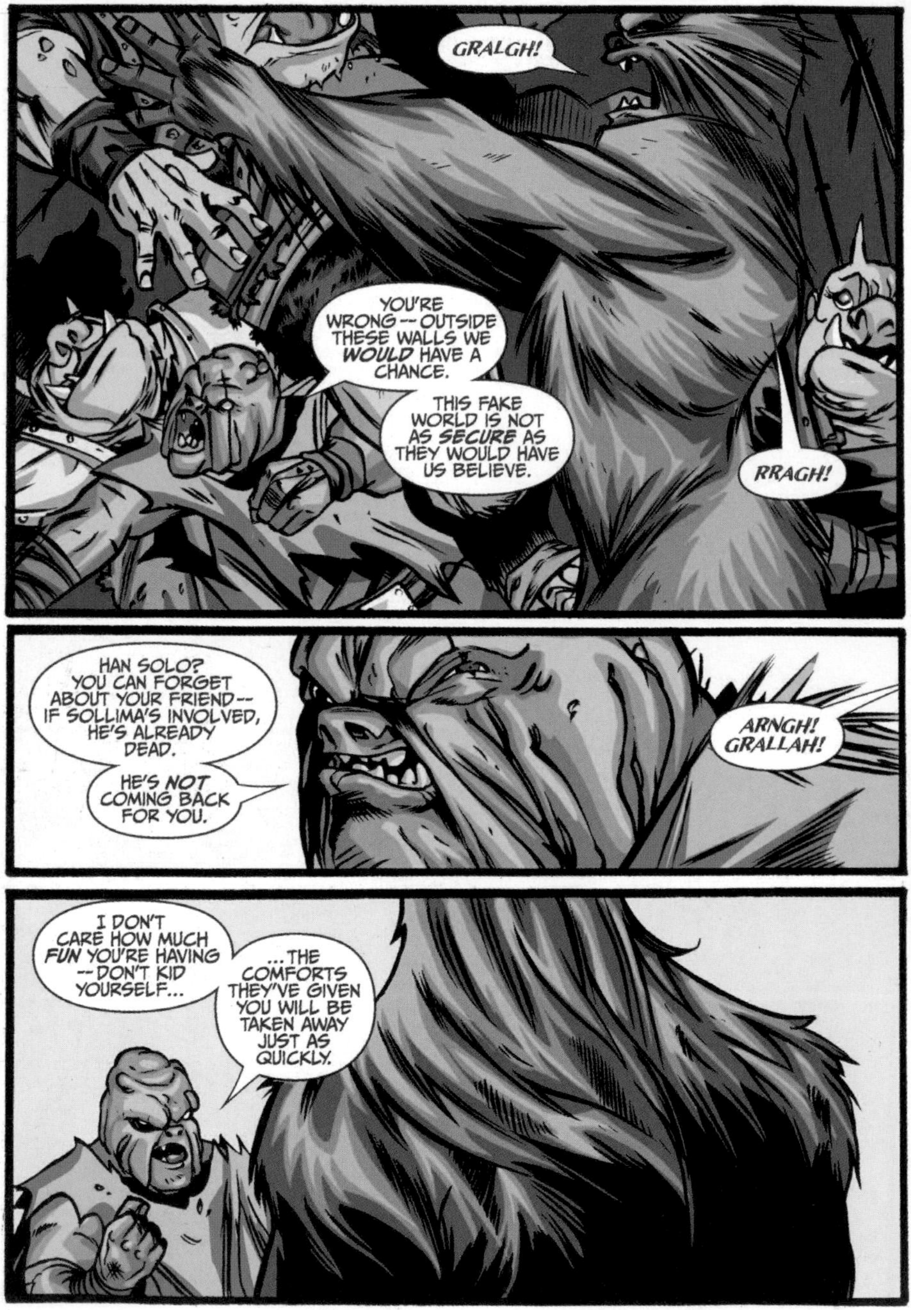
GRALGH!
YOU'RE WRONG -- OUTSIDE THESE WALLS WE WOULD HAVE A CHANCE.
THIS FAKE WORLD IS NOT AS SECURE AS THEY WOULD HAVE US BELIEVE.
RRAGH!
HAN SOLO? YOU CAN FORGET ABOUT YOUR FRIEND-- IF SOLLIMA'S INVOLVED, HE'S ALREADY DEAD.
HE'S NOT COMING BACK FOR YOU.
ARNGH! GRALLAH!
I DON'T CARE HOW MUCH FUN YOU'RE HAVING --DON'T KID YOURSELF...
...THE COMFORTS THEY'VE GIVEN YOU WILL BE TAKEN AWAY JUST AS QUICKLY.

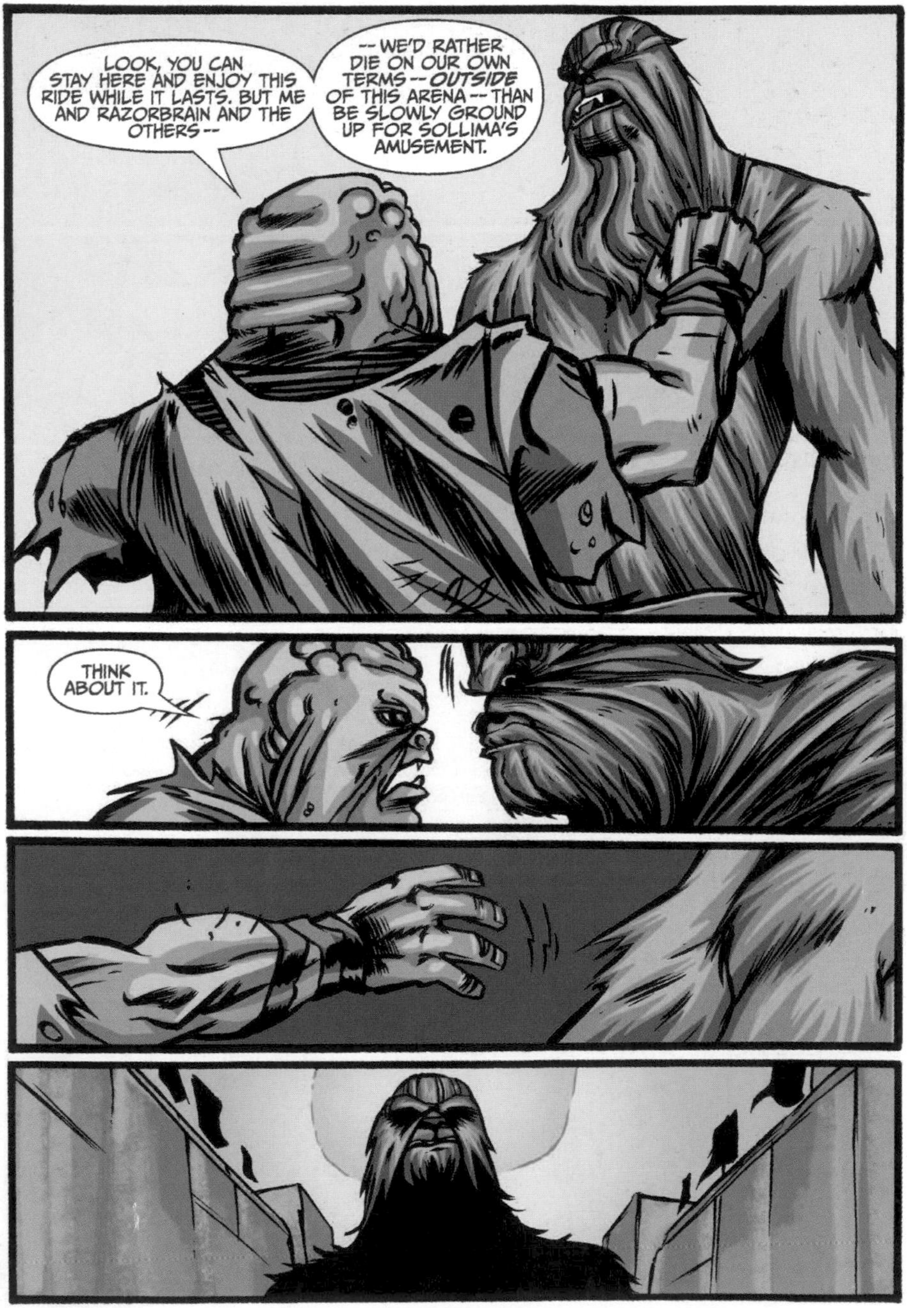
LOOK, YOU CAN STAY HERE AND ENJOY THIS RIDE WHILE IT LASTS. BUT ME AND RAZORBRAIN AND THE OTHERS --
-- WE'D RATHER DIE ON OUR OWN TERMS -- OUTSIDE OF THIS ARENA -- THAN BE SLOWLY GROUND UP FOR SOLLIMA'S AMUSEMENT.
THINK ABOUT IT.

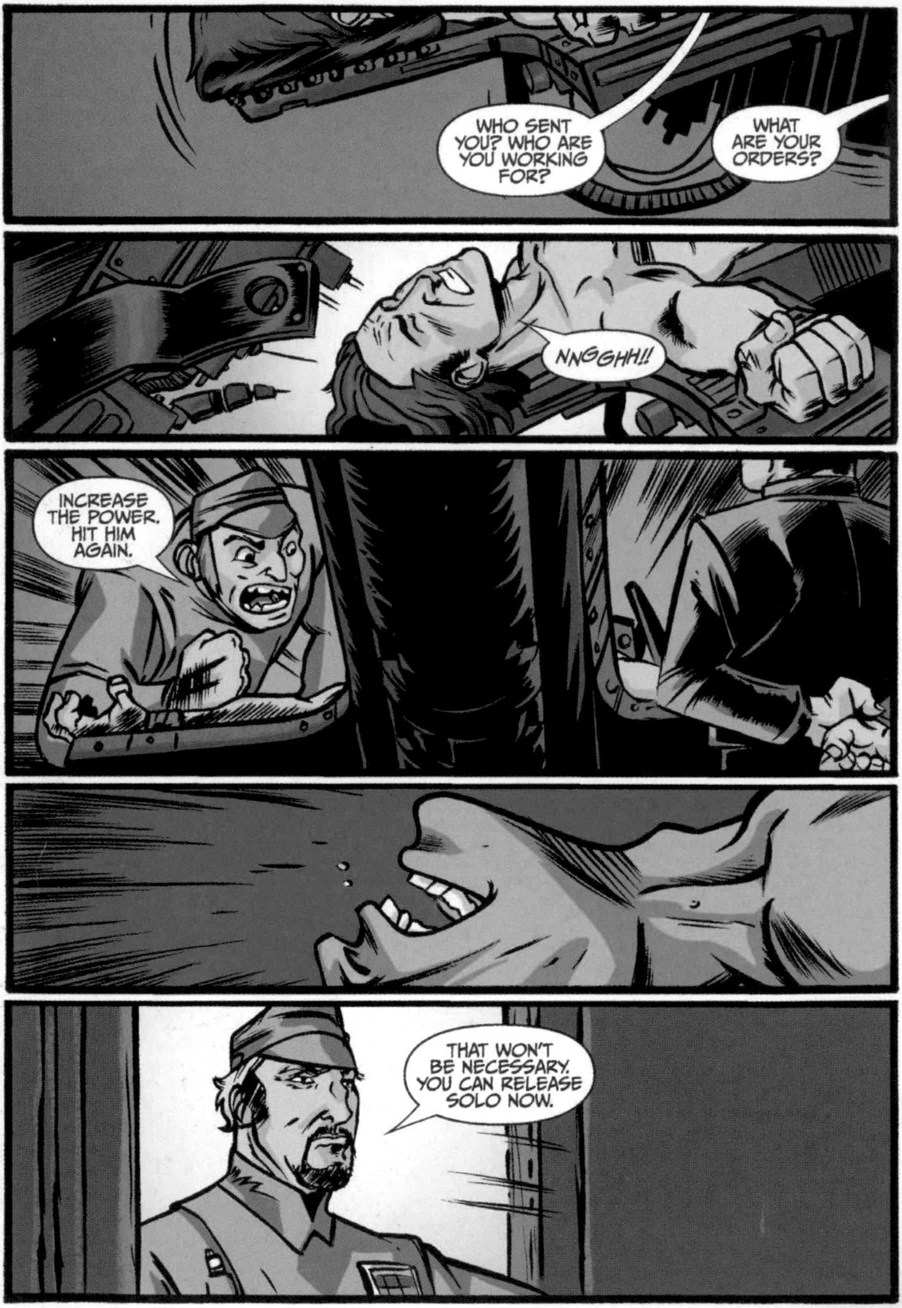
WHO SENT YOU? WHO ARE YOU WORKING FOR?
WHAT ARE YOUR ORDERS?
NNGGHH!!
INCREASE THE POWER. HIT HIM AGAIN.
THAT WON'T BE NECESSARY. YOU CAN RELEASE SOLO NOW.

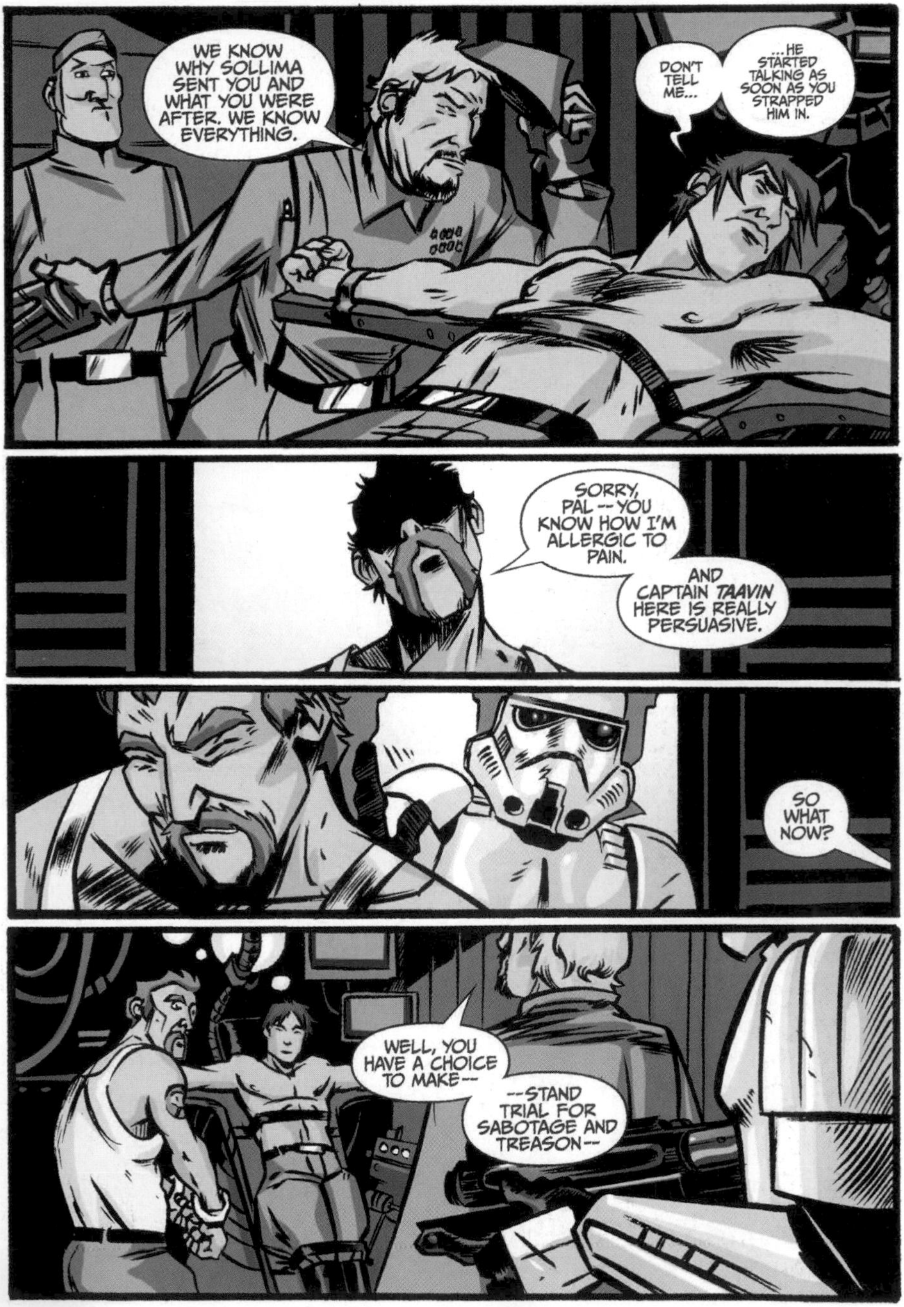
WE KNOW WHY SOLLIMA SENT YOU AND WHAT YOU WERE AFTER. WE KNOW EVERYTHING.
DON'T TELL ME...
...HE STARTED TALKING AS SOON AS YOU STRAPPED HIM IN.
SORRY, PAL--YOU KNOW HOW I'M ALLERGIC TO PAIN.
AND CAPTAIN TAAVIN HERE IS REALLY PERSUASIVE.
SO WHAT NOW?
WELL, YOU HAVE A CHOICE TO MAKE--
--STAND TRIAL FOR SABOTAGE AND TREASON--

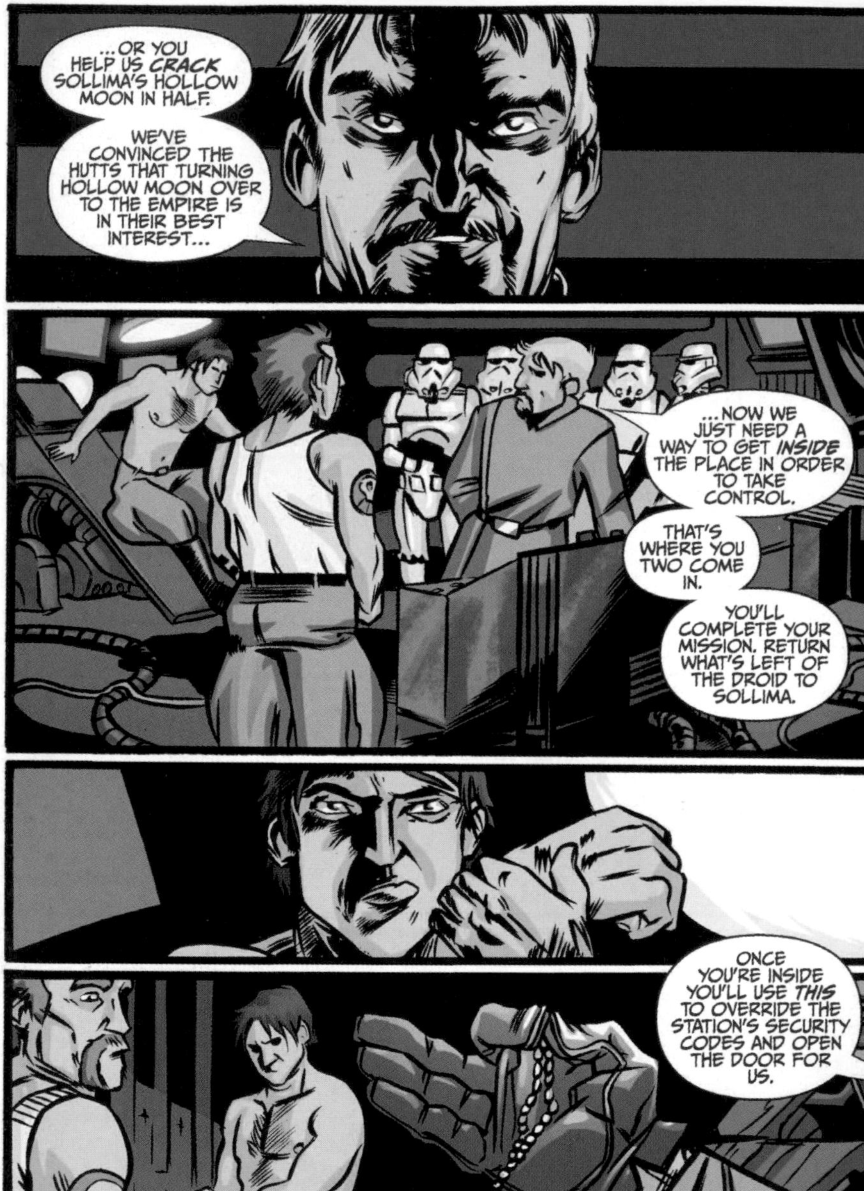
...OR YOU HELP US CRACK SOLLIMA'S HOLLOW MOON IN HALF.
WE'VE CONVINCED THE HUTTS THAT TURNING HOLLOW MOON OVER TO THE EMPIRE IS IN THEIR BEST INTEREST...
...NOW WE JUST NEED A WAY TO GET INSIDE THE PLACE IN ORDER TO TAKE CONTROL.
THAT'S WHERE YOU TWO COME IN.
YOU'LL COMPLETE YOUR MISSION. RETURN WHAT'S LEFT OF THE DROID TO SOLLIMA.
ONCE YOU'RE INSIDE YOU'LL USE THIS TO OVERRIDE THE STATION'S SECURITY CODES AND OPEN THE DOOR FOR US.

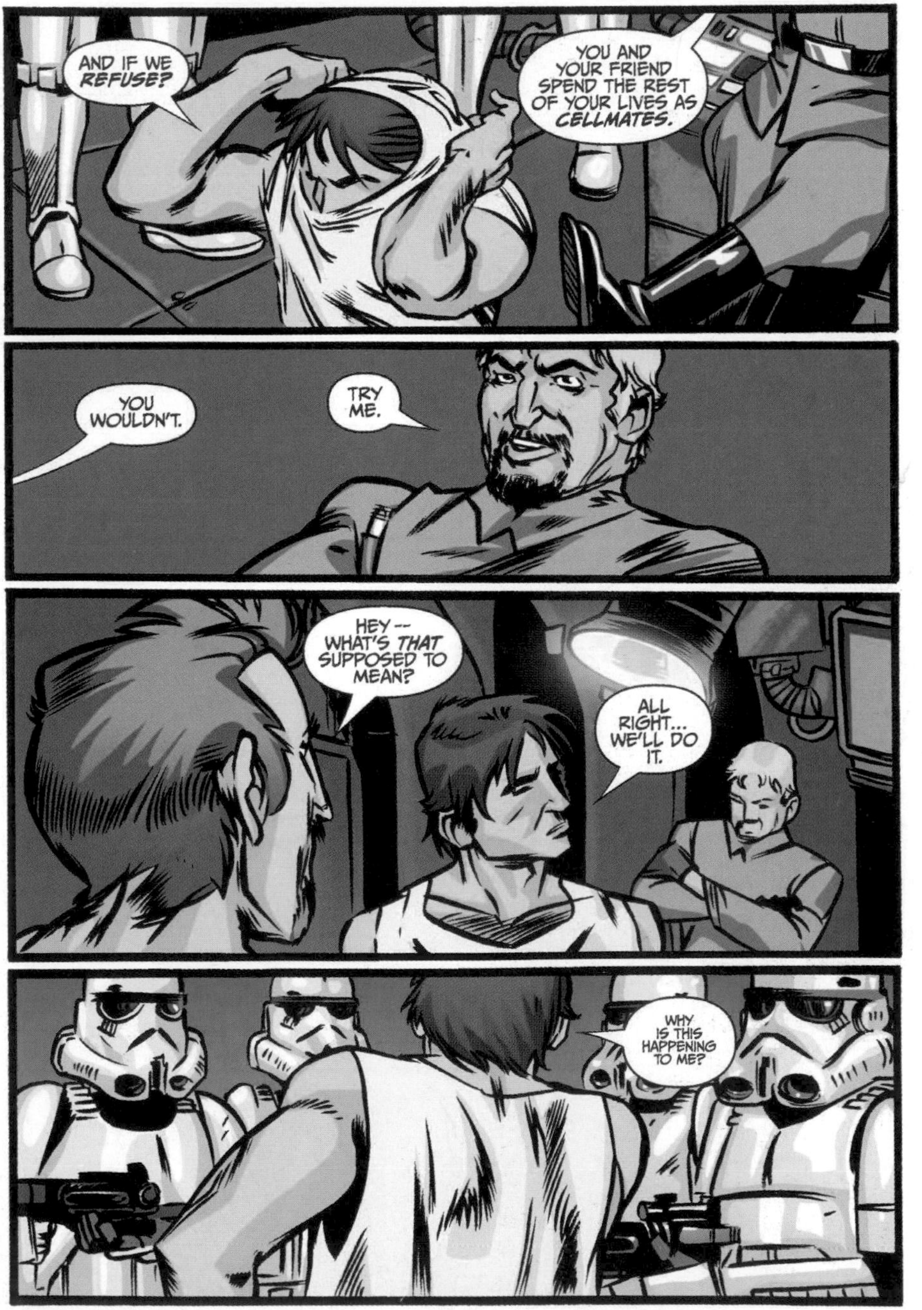
AND IF WE *REFUSE?*
YOU AND YOUR FRIEND SPEND THE REST OF YOUR LIVES AS *CELLMATES.*
YOU WOULDN'T.
TRY ME.
HEY -- WHAT'S *THAT* SUPPOSED TO MEAN?
ALL RIGHT... WE'LL DO IT.
WHY IS THIS HAPPENING TO ME?

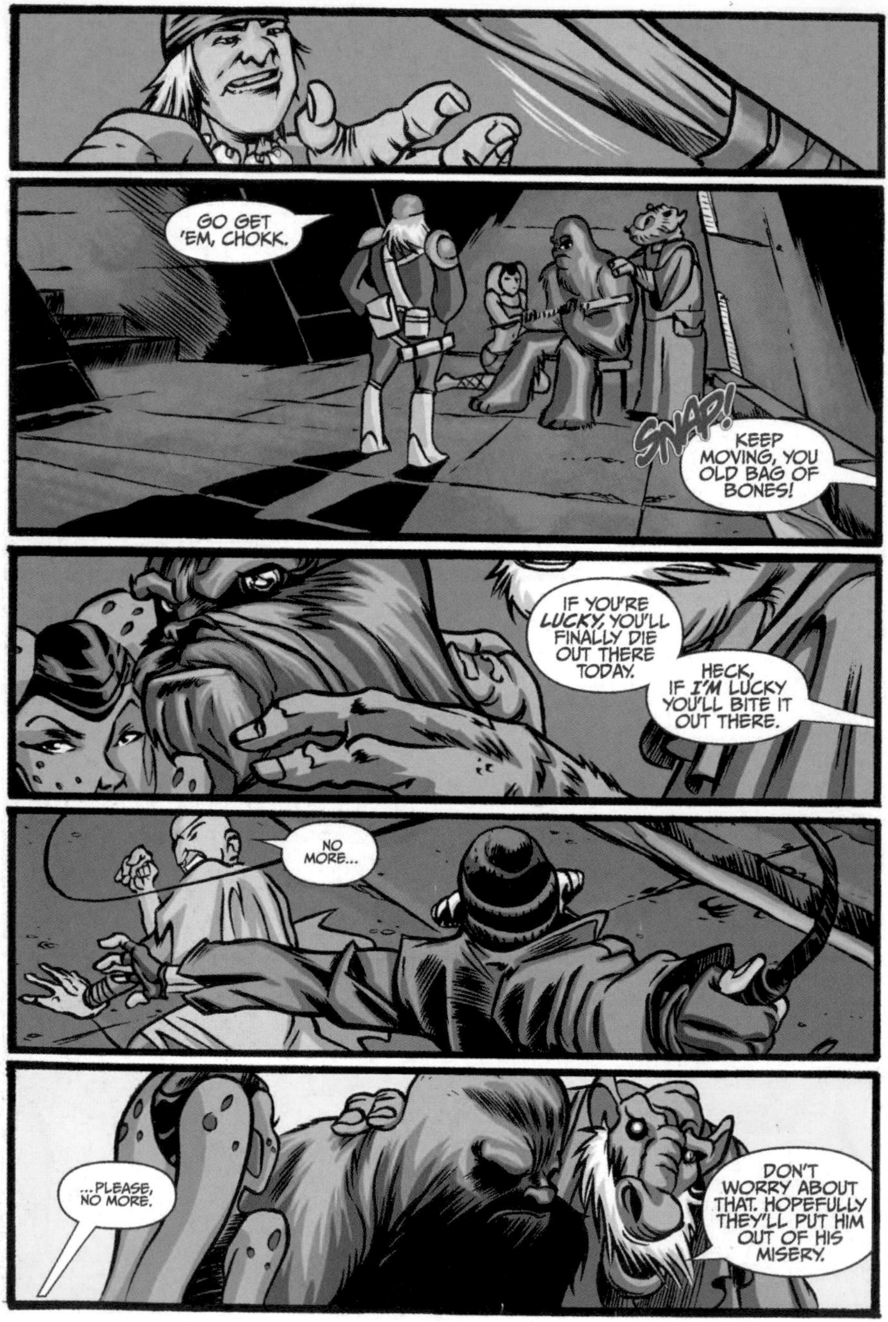
GO GET 'EM, CHOKK.
SNAP!
KEEP MOVING, YOU OLD BAG OF BONES!
IF YOU'RE LUCKY, YOU'LL FINALLY DIE OUT THERE TODAY.
HECK, IF I'M LUCKY YOU'LL BITE IT OUT THERE.
NO MORE...
...PLEASE, NO MORE.
DON'T WORRY ABOUT THAT. HOPEFULLY THEY'LL PUT HIM OUT OF HIS MISERY.

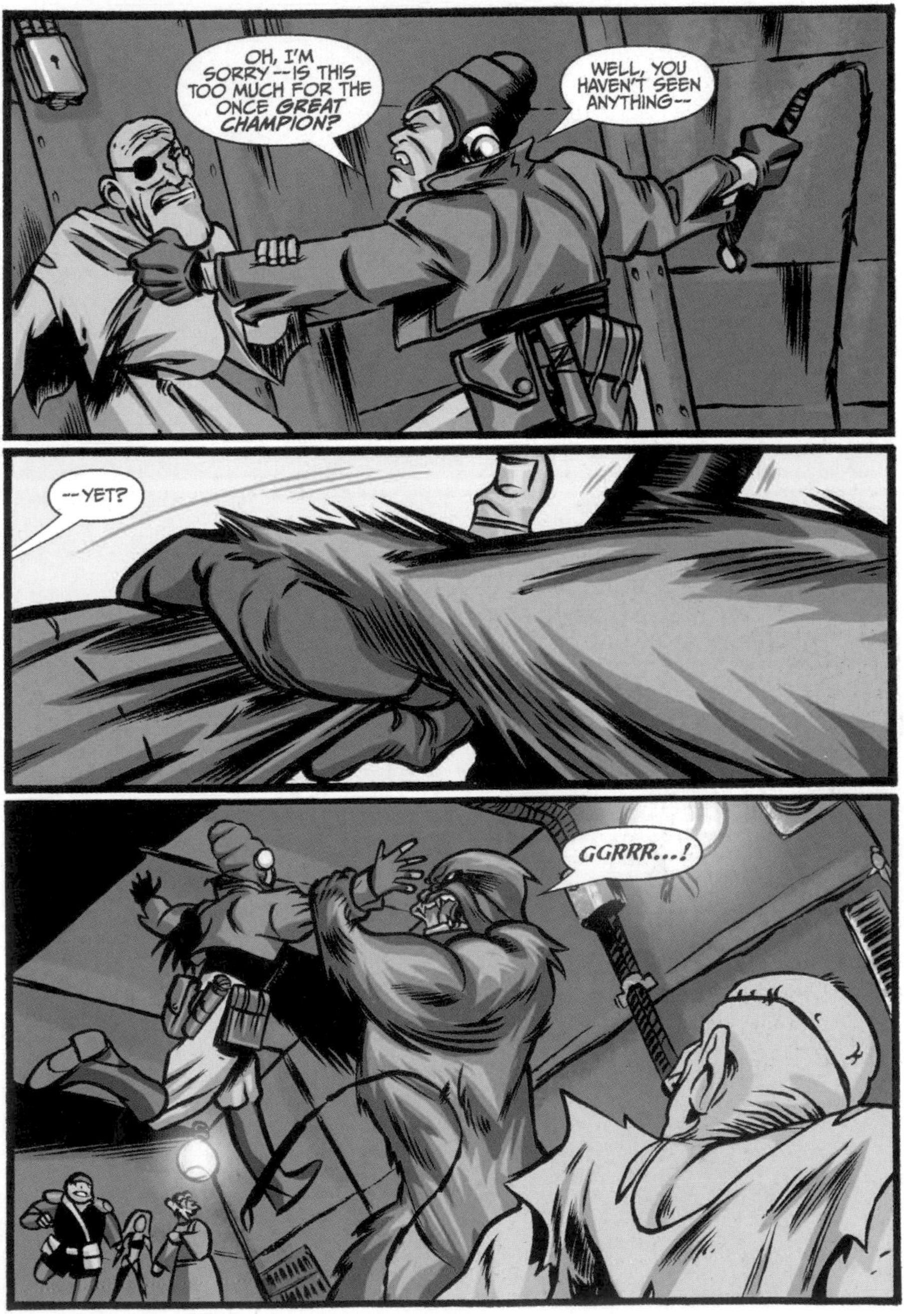
OH, I'M SORRY --IS THIS TOO MUCH FOR THE ONCE GREAT CHAMPION?
WELL, YOU HAVEN'T SEEN ANYTHING--
--YET?
GGRRR...!

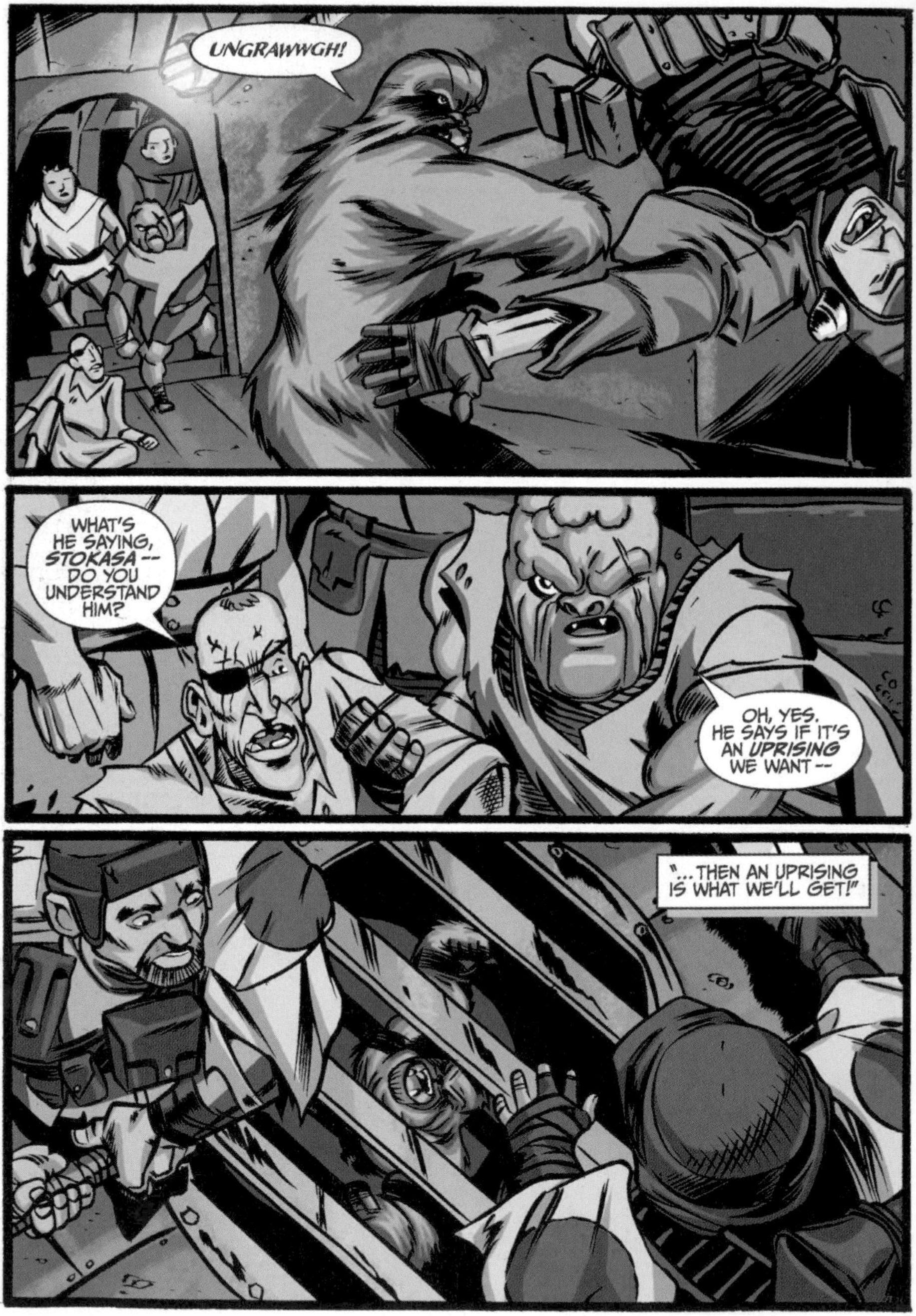
UNGRAWWGH!
WHAT'S HE SAYING, STOKASA -- DO YOU UNDERSTAND HIM?
OH, YES. HE SAYS IF IT'S AN UPRISING WE WANT --
"...THEN AN UPRISING IS WHAT WE'LL GET!"

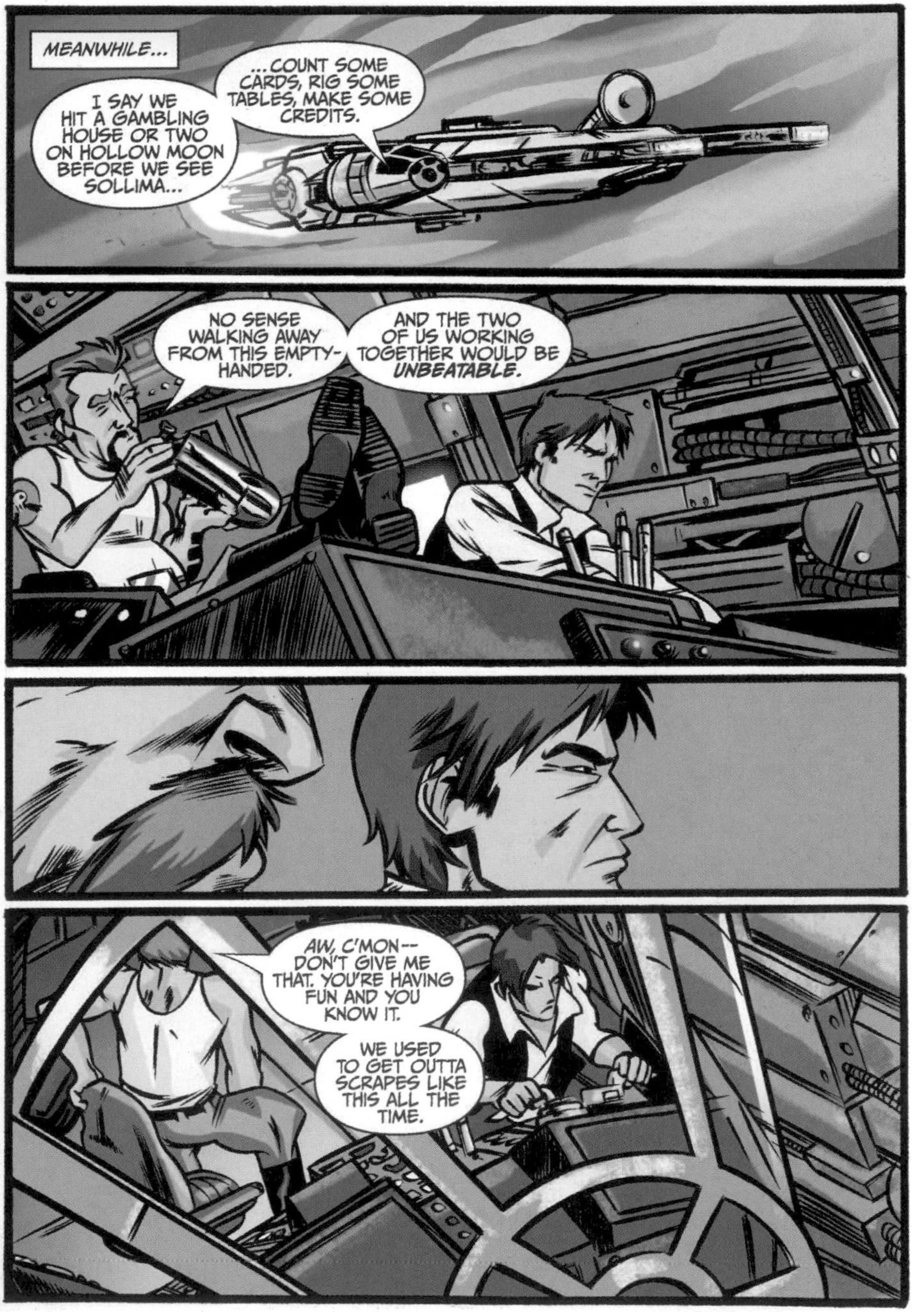
MEANWHILE...
I SAY WE HIT A GAMBLING HOUSE OR TWO ON HOLLOW MOON BEFORE WE SEE SOLLIMA...
...COUNT SOME CARDS, RIG SOME TABLES, MAKE SOME CREDITS.
NO SENSE WALKING AWAY FROM THIS EMPTY-HANDED.
AND THE TWO OF US WORKING TOGETHER WOULD BE *UNBEATABLE.*
AW, C'MON-- DON'T GIVE ME THAT. YOU'RE HAVING FUN AND YOU KNOW IT.
WE USED TO GET OUTTA SCRAPES LIKE THIS ALL THE TIME.

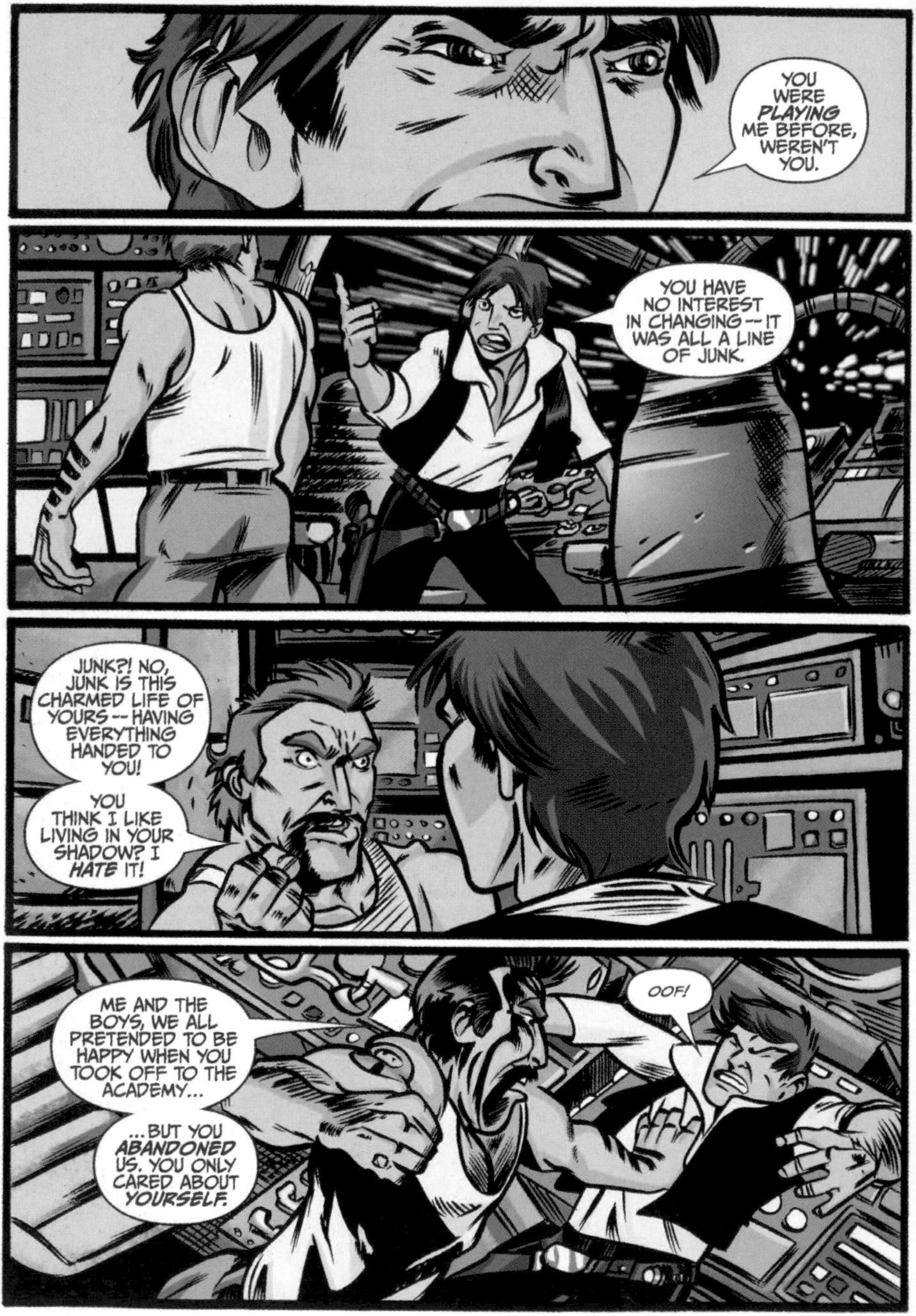
YOU WERE PLAYING ME BEFORE, WEREN'T YOU.
YOU HAVE NO INTEREST IN CHANGING -- IT WAS ALL A LINE OF JUNK.
JUNK?! NO, JUNK IS THIS CHARMED LIFE OF YOURS -- HAVING EVERYTHING HANDED TO YOU!
YOU THINK I LIKE LIVING IN YOUR SHADOW? I HATE IT!
ME AND THE BOYS, WE ALL PRETENDED TO BE HAPPY WHEN YOU TOOK OFF TO THE ACADEMY...
OOF!
...BUT YOU ABANDONED US. YOU ONLY CARED ABOUT YOURSELF.

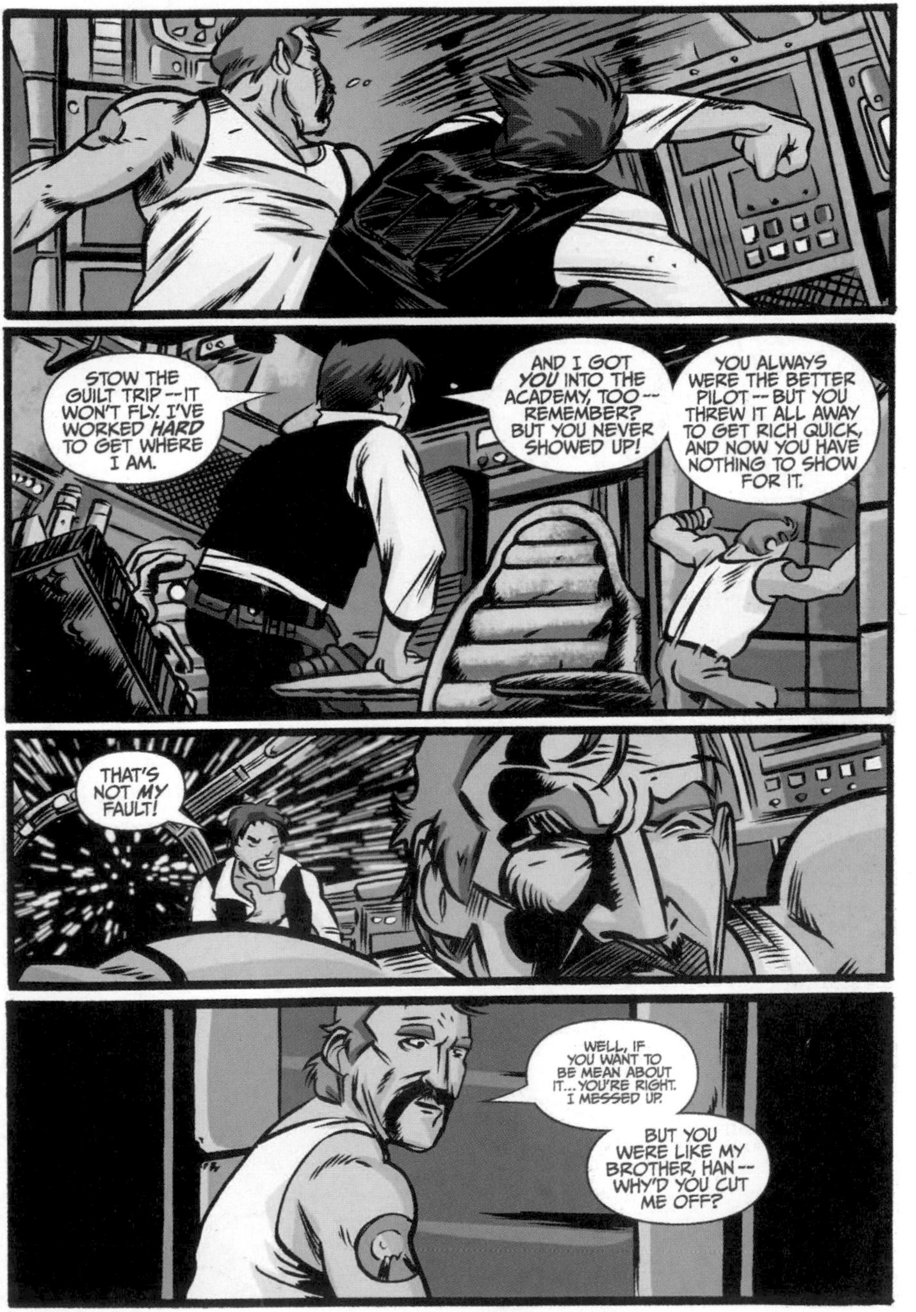
STOW THE GUILT TRIP --IT WON'T FLY. I'VE WORKED HARD TO GET WHERE I AM.
AND I GOT YOU INTO THE ACADEMY, TOO-- REMEMBER? BUT YOU NEVER SHOWED UP!
YOU ALWAYS WERE THE BETTER PILOT -- BUT YOU THREW IT ALL AWAY TO GET RICH QUICK, AND NOW YOU HAVE NOTHING TO SHOW FOR IT.
THAT'S NOT MY FAULT!
WELL, IF YOU WANT TO BE MEAN ABOUT IT... YOU'RE RIGHT. I MESSED UP.
BUT YOU WERE LIKE MY BROTHER, HAN -- WHY'D YOU CUT ME OFF?

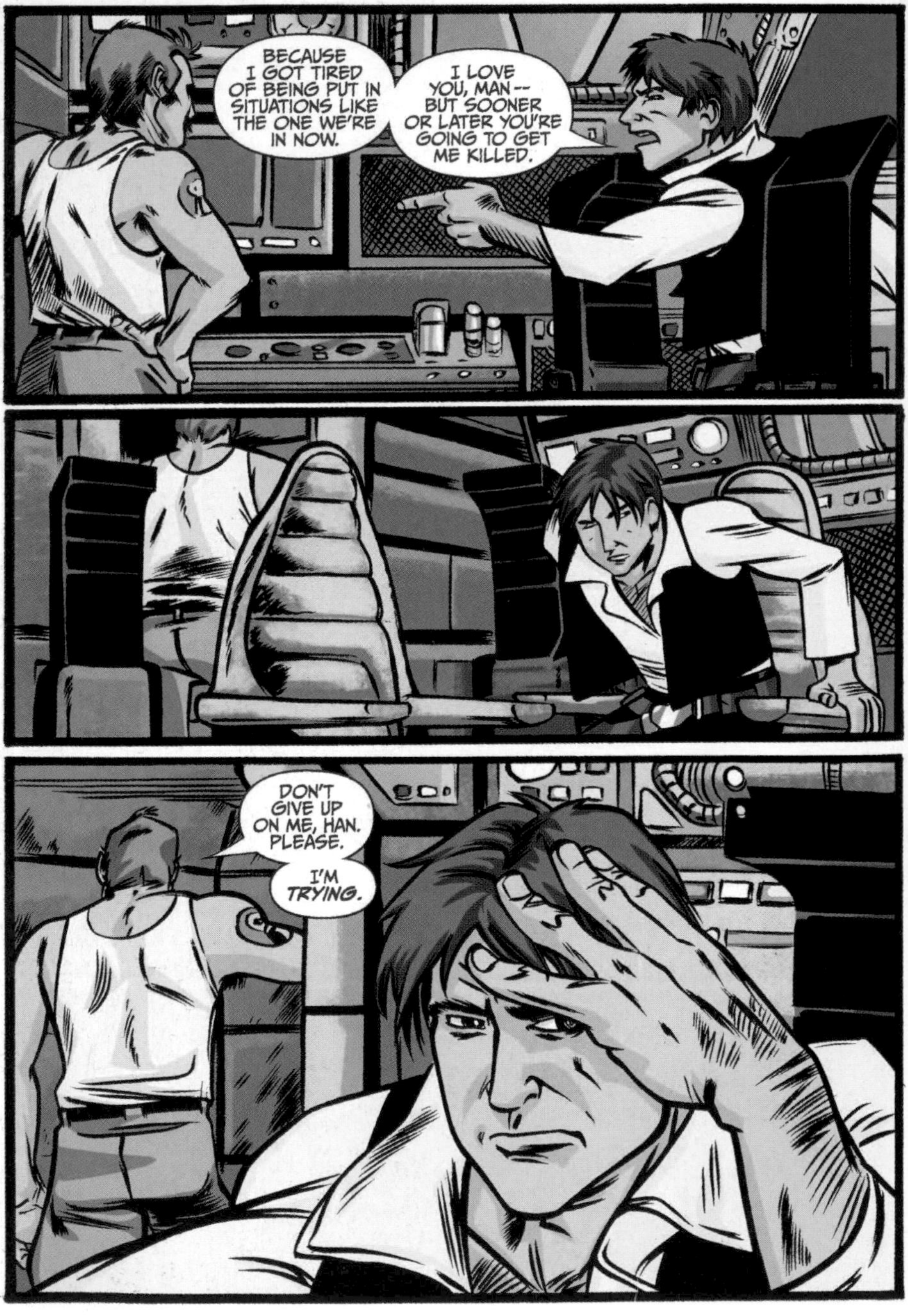
BECAUSE I GOT TIRED OF BEING PUT IN SITUATIONS LIKE THE ONE WE'RE IN NOW.
I LOVE YOU, MAN-- BUT SOONER OR LATER YOU'RE GOING TO GET ME KILLED.
DON'T GIVE UP ON ME, HAN. PLEASE.
I'M *TRYING*.

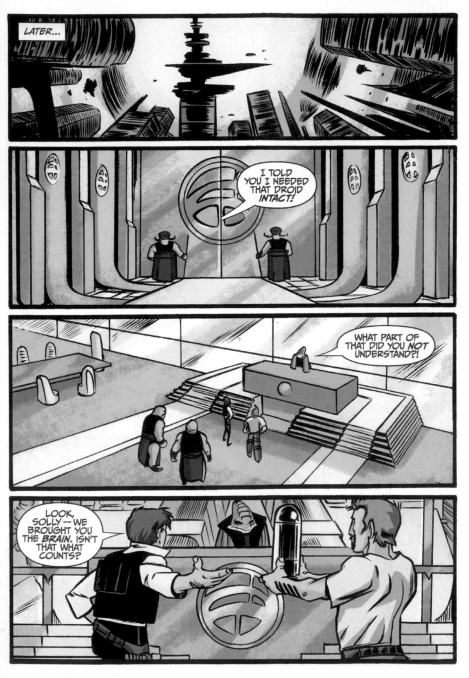

LATER...

I TOLD YOU I NEEDED THAT DROID *INTACT!*

WHAT PART OF THAT DID YOU *NOT* UNDERSTAND?!

LOOK, SOLLY -- WE BROUGHT YOU THE *BRAIN.* ISN'T THAT WHAT COUNTS?

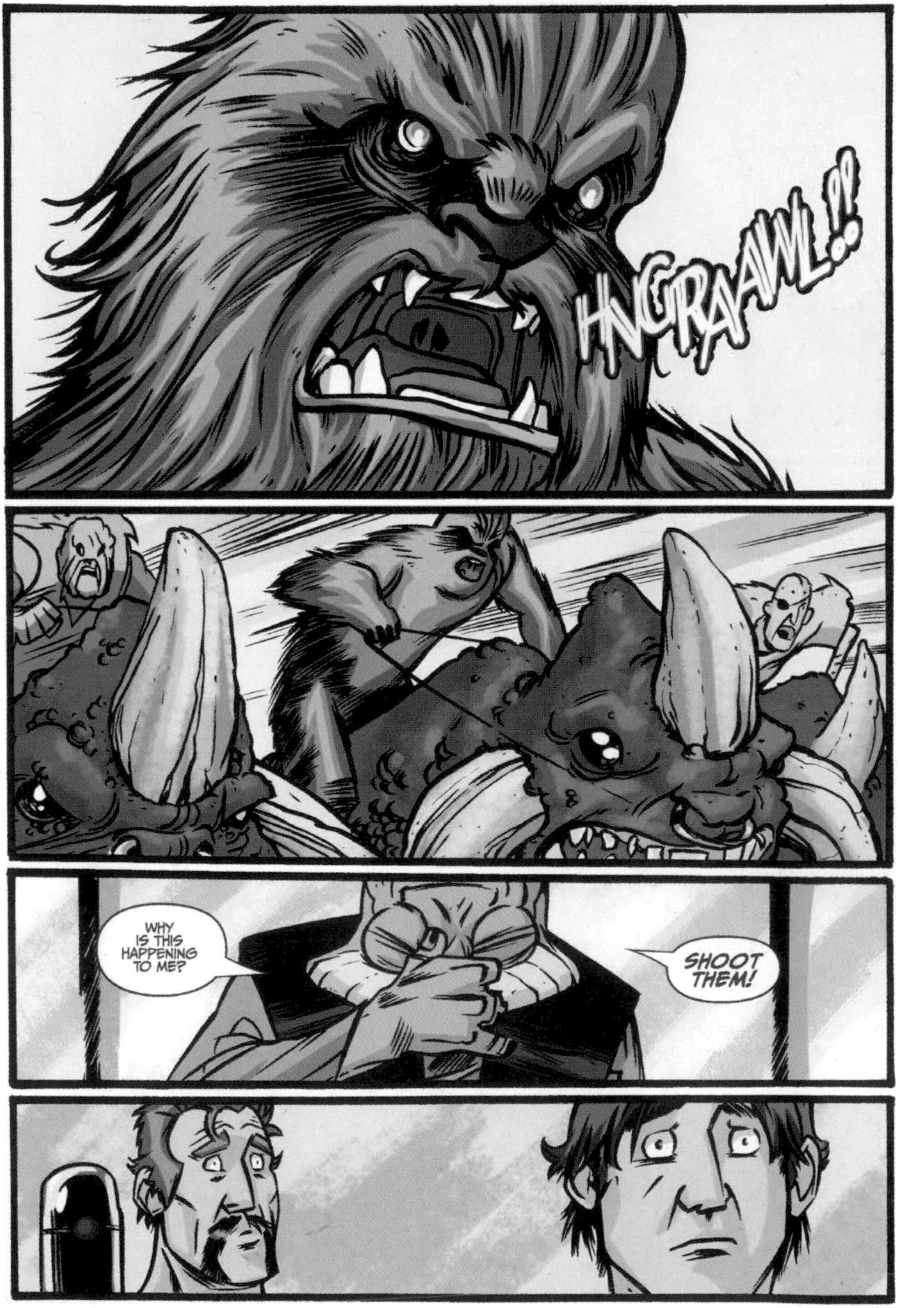
HNGRAAWL!?!
WHY IS THIS HAPPENING TO ME?
SHOOT THEM!

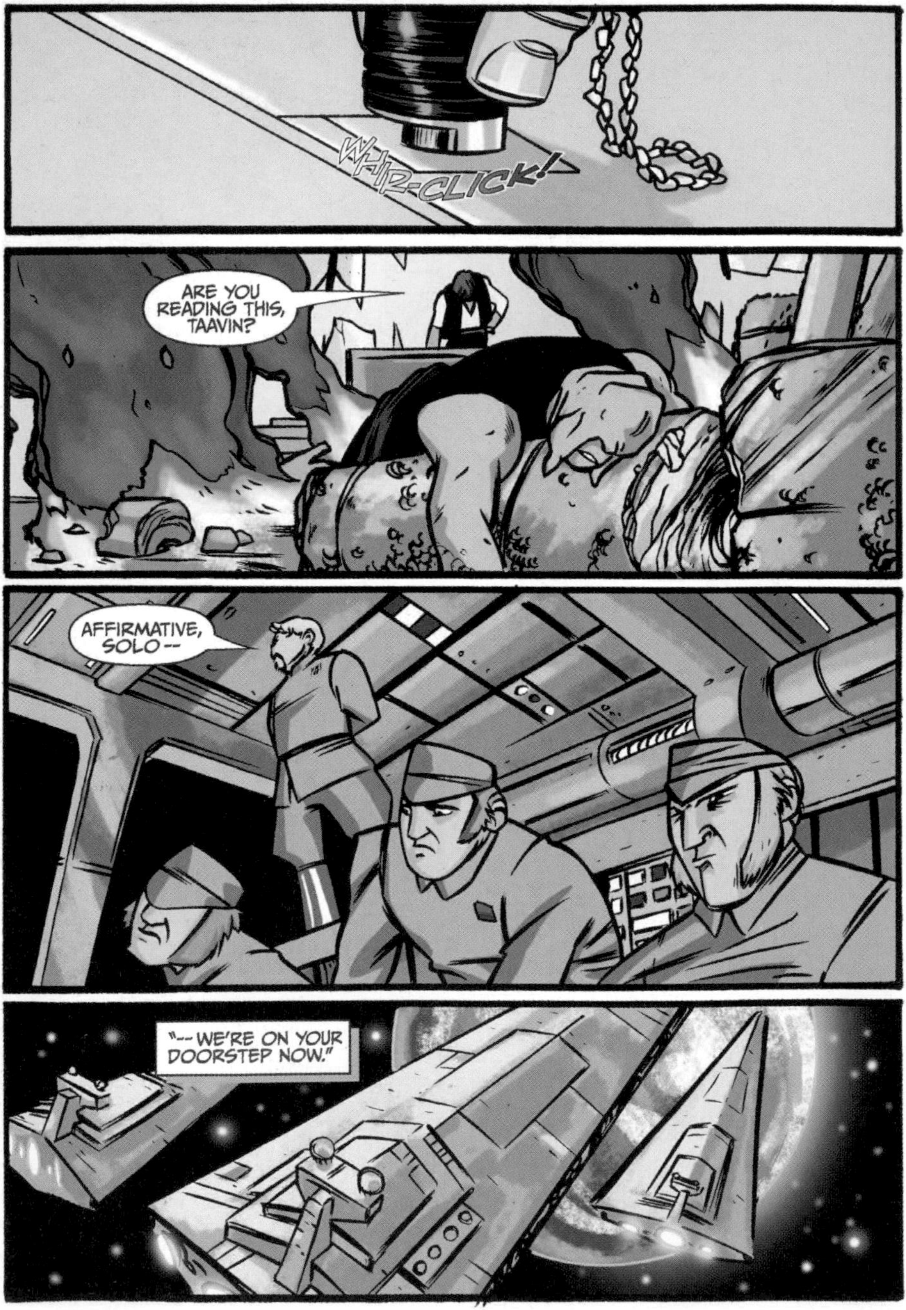
WHIR-CLICK!
ARE YOU READING THIS, TAAVIN?
AFFIRMATIVE, SOLO --
"-- WE'RE ON YOUR DOORSTEP NOW."

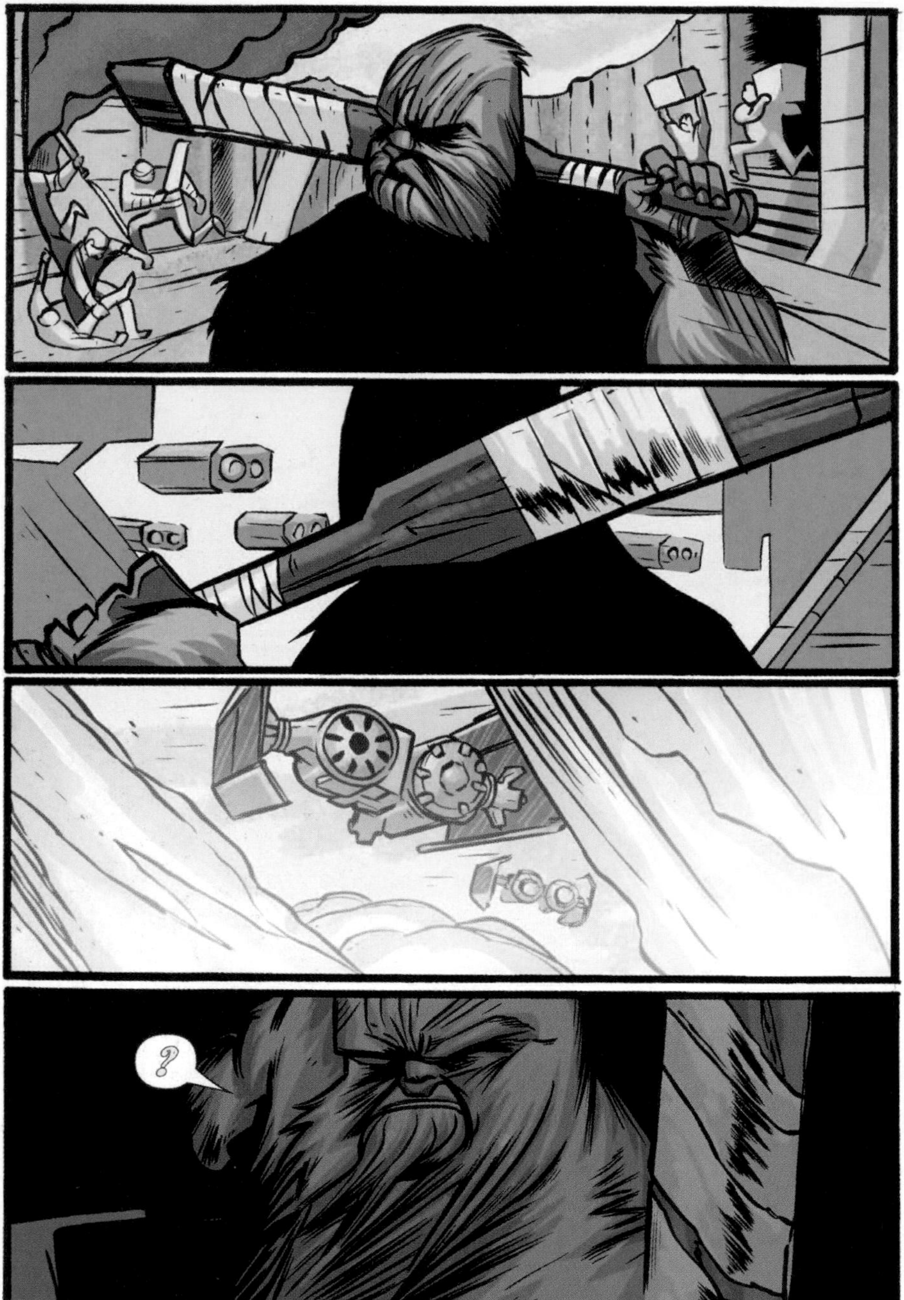
?

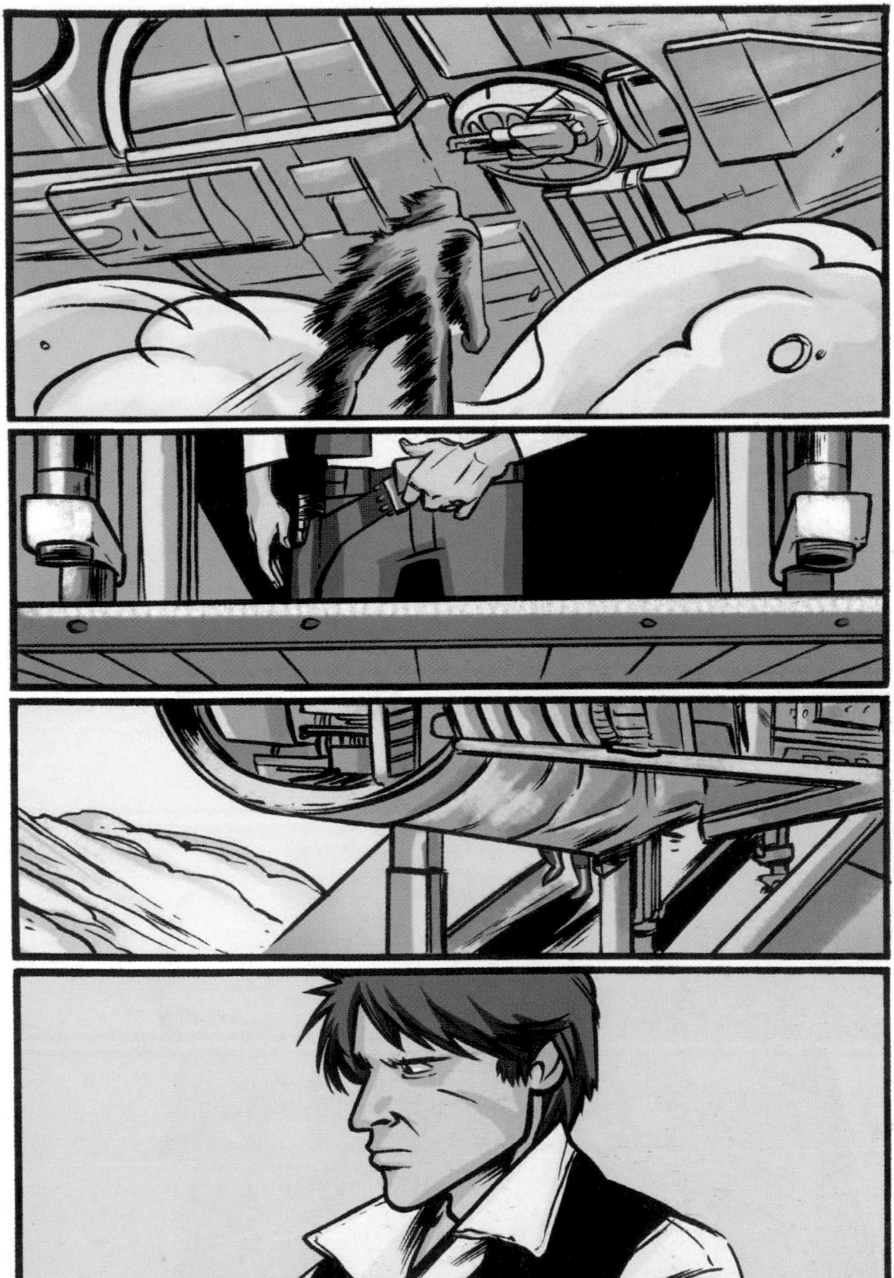

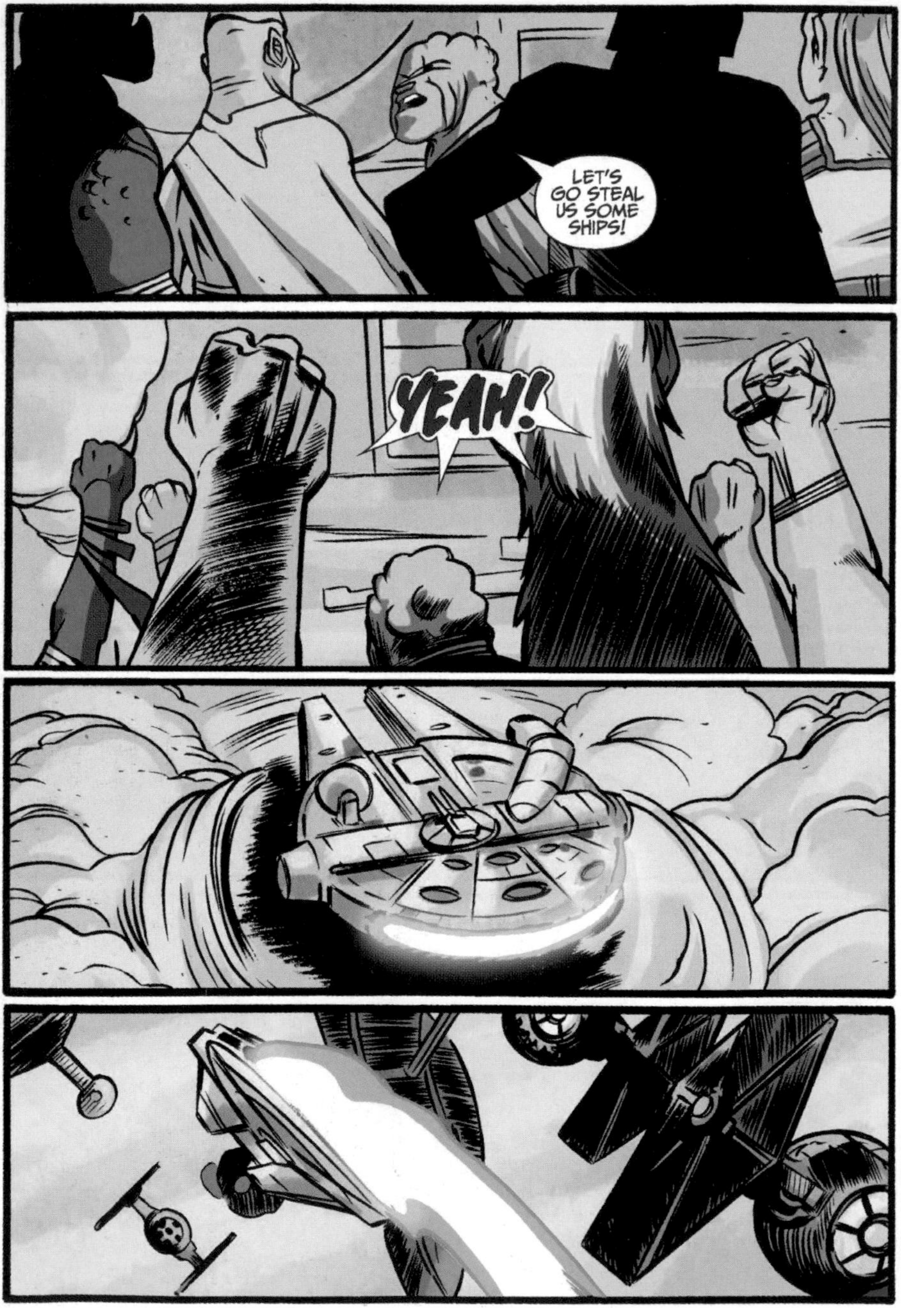
LET'S GO STEAL US SOME SHIPS!
YEAH!

65

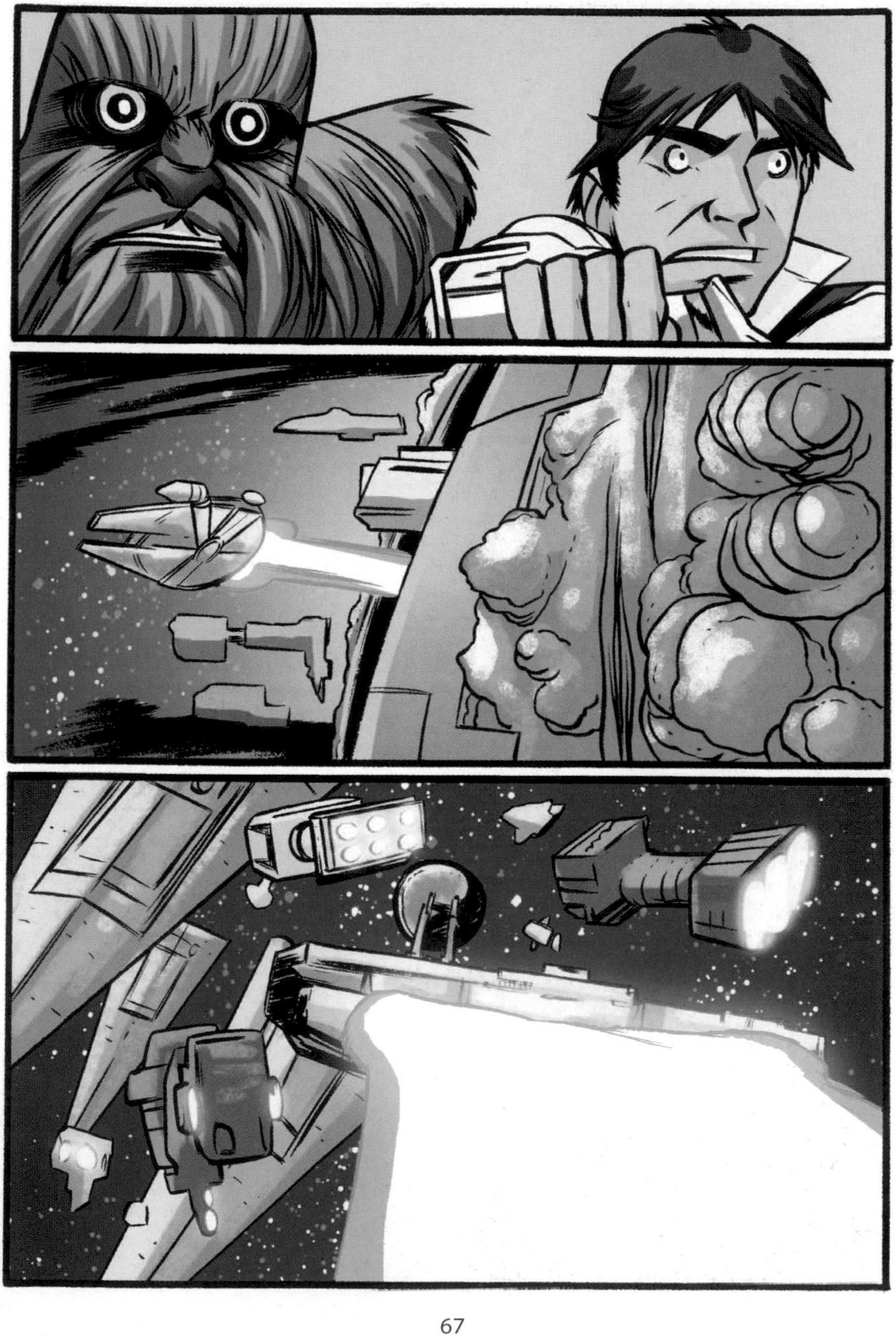

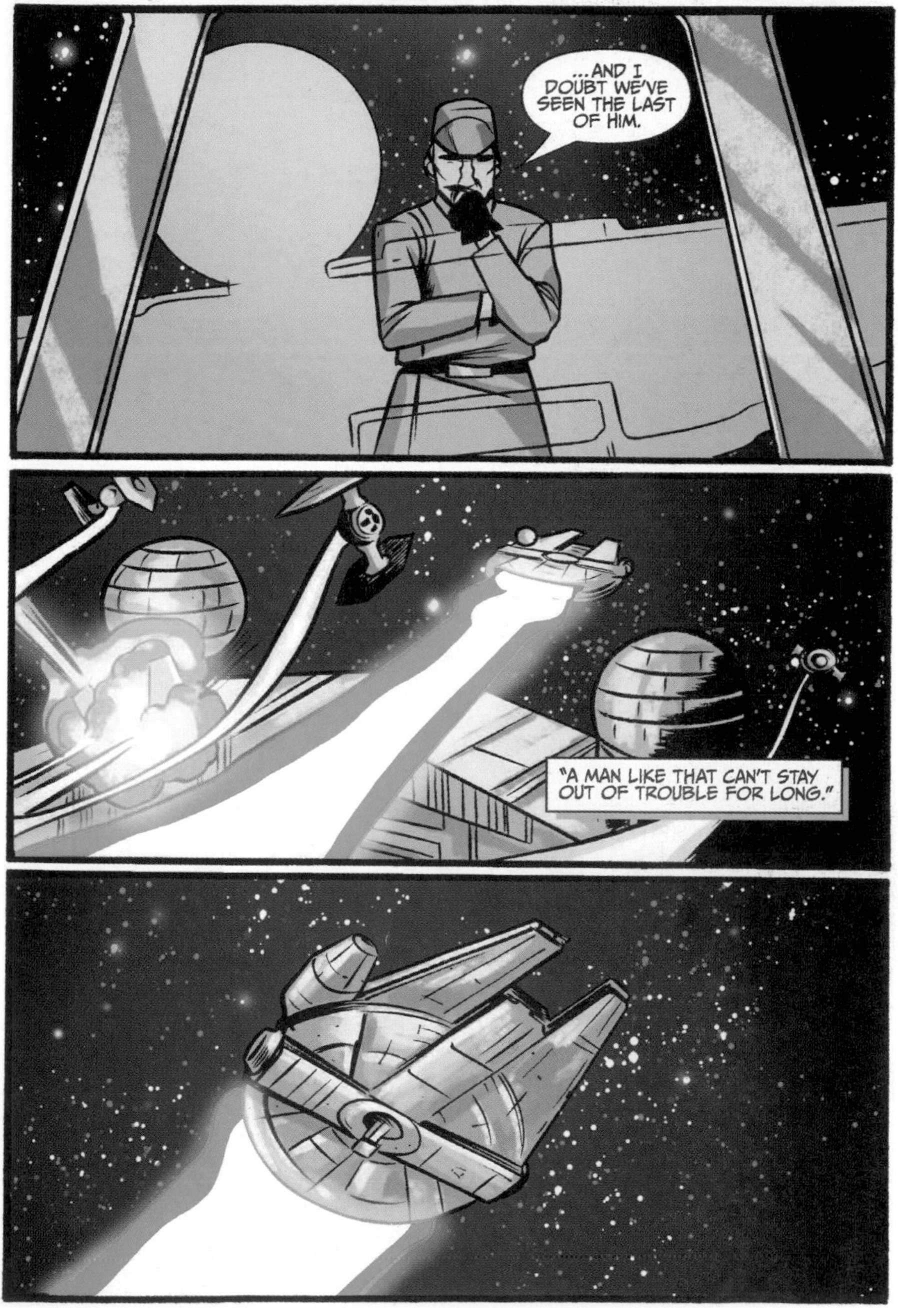
...AND I DOUBT WE'VE SEEN THE LAST OF HIM.
"A MAN LIKE THAT CAN'T STAY OUT OF TROUBLE FOR LONG."

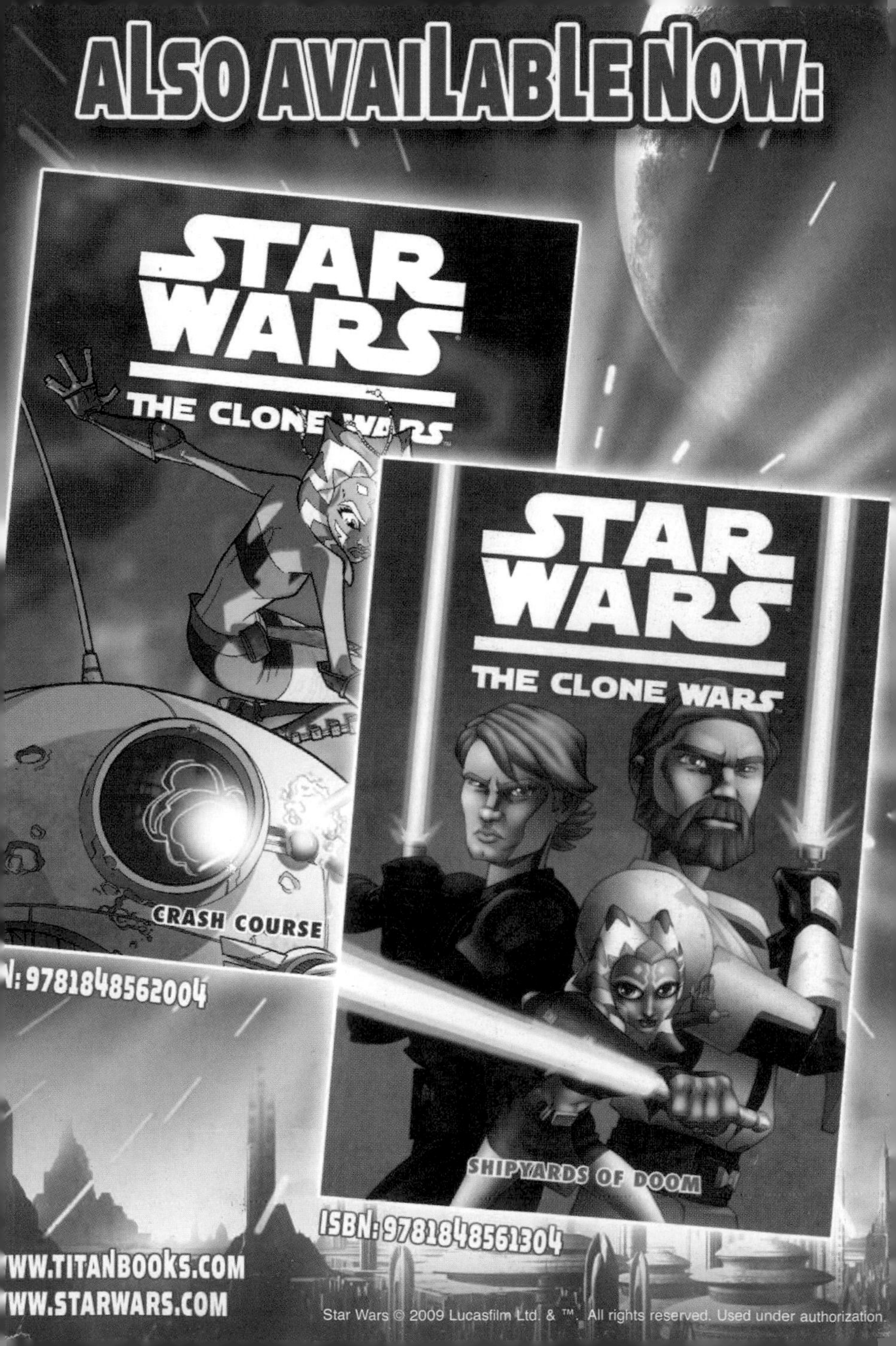
ALSO AVAILABLE NOW:
STAR WARS
THE CLONE WARS
CRASH COURSE
N: 9781848562004
STAR WARS
THE CLONE WARS
SHIPYARDS OF DOOM
ISBN: 9781848561304
WW.TITANBOOKS.COM
WW.STARWARS.COM
Star Wars © 2009 Lucasfilm Ltd. & ™. All rights reserved. Used under authorization.

THE FORCE IS

www.titanbooks.com

DON'T MISS THE CONTINUING BATTLE AGAIN!
CLONE WARS